Post-9/11 Espionage Fiction in the US and Pakistan

As the events of 11 September 2001 and their aftermath influence new developments in spy fiction as a popular genre, an examination of these literary narratives concerned with espionage and terrorism can reshape our approach to non-fictive representations of the same concerns.

Post-9/11 Espionage Fiction in the US and Pakistan examines post-9/11 American spy fictions alongside Pakistani novels that draw upon many of the same figures, tropes, and conventions. As the Pakistani texts re-place spy fiction's conventions, they offer another vantage point from which to view the affective appeals common to these conventions' usual deployment in American texts. This book argues that the appropriation by Pakistani writers of these conventions insistently tracks how the formulaic and popular nature of post-9/11 American espionage thrillers forwards and reinforces "appropriate" affective responses, often linked to domestic sites and relations, to "terrorism." It also analyzes and compares American and Pakistani representations of the twinned figures of the spy (or his proxy) and the "terrorist," a term frequently conflated with fundamentalist. The insights of these analyses can serve as interpretive interruptions of non-fictive representations of Pakistani–US "war on terror" relations.

Offering an innovative analysis of the reflection of narrative conventions in our view of the real-life events, this book will attract scholars with an interest in Pakistani literature, postcolonial literature, Asian Studies and Terrorism Studies.

Cara Cilano is Professor of English at the University of North Carolina Wilmington, USA. She is author of *Contemporary Pakistani Fiction in English: Idea, Nation, State* (Routledge, 2013), and *National Identities in Pakistan: The 1971 War in Contemporary Pakistani Fiction* (Routledge, 2010), as well as editor of *From Solidarity to Schisms: 9/11 and After in Fiction and Film from Outside the US* (2009).

Routledge Contemporary South Asia Series

Post-9/11 Espionage Fiction in the US and Pakistan

Spies and "terrorists"

Cara Cilano

 Routledge
Taylor & Francis Group

LONDON AND NEW YORK

First published 2014
by Routledge
2 Park Square, Milton Park, Abingdon, Oxon OX14 4RN

and by Routledge
711 Third Avenue, New York, NY 10017

Routledge is an imprint of the Taylor & Francis Group, an informa business

© 2014 Cara Cilano

British Library Cataloguing in Publication Data
A catalogue record for this book is available from the British Library

Library of Congress Cataloging in Publication Data
Cilano, Cara.
Post-9/11 espionage fiction in the US and Pakistan : spies and "terrorists" / Cara Cilano.
  pages cm. -- (Routledge contemporary South Asia series)
Includes bibliographical references and index.
1. Spy stories, American--History and criticism. 2. Pakistani fiction (English)--History and criticism. 3. American fiction--21st century--History and criticism. 4. Pakistani fiction (English)--21st century--History and criticism. 5. Spies in literature. 6. Espionage in literature. I. Title.
  PS374.S764C55 2014
  813'.087209--dc23
    2013049196

ISBN: 978-0-415-68451-4 (hbk)
ISBN: 978-1-315-77020-8 (ebk)

Typeset in Times New Roman
by Taylor & Francis Books

Printed and bound by CPI Group (UK) Ltd, Croydon, CR0 4YY

to Lisa,
who's always been my hero

Contents

Acknowledgments

In fulfillment of a promise made to three different classes over the course of three different semesters, I extend my warm gratitude to my students in the senior seminar in spring 2010, the honors course in fall 2011, and the graduate seminar in fall 2012. With unmatched curiosity and patience, these students—ranging from first year undergraduates to last semester MA students—enthusiastically examined spies, fundamentalists, terrorists, survivalists, affect theorists, and more right along with me. I hope they hear the echo of their own questions in what I'm asking in these pages.

Similarly, I want to thank the University of North Carolina Wilmington's Graduate English Association for inviting me to deliver the plenary talk at two of their annual conferences. These opportunities prompted me to articulate emergent lines of thought and then motivated me to write, write, write.

Participants at the 2012 South Asia Conference in Madison, WI, as well as Claire Chambers and Caroline Herbert, gave me the chance to think through related ideas, and those experiences enriched my thinking about the issues I discuss here.

Once again, I find myself in the debt of Dorothea Schaefter and Jillian Morrison at Routledge. I am fortunate that they have taken an interest in the work that I do, and I've benefited immensely from their hard work, as well.

In addition to talking through many of the claims I make in the following pages, my friend Lee Schweninger served as my +1 at more espionage films than I can remember. His encouragement and genuine interest have made this project a great adventure for me.

Over the years I've taken to pursue this research and writing, the Cilano ranks have swelled dramatically. Benjamin, Nicholas, Vincenzo, and Carolyn add to the joy Sammy, Sofia, and Max have always brought. I've been grateful, too, for the interest in my work that my parents and siblings have shown and even more for their patience when my writing has meant limited time with them.

Every now and then, I can get my mom to tell the story of how my sister Lisa anticipated the arrival of a baby sister. Poor thing had to suffer through the addition of two more brothers before I made my entrance. There's no way to say what it's meant to me to be anticipated with such excitement by her. Lisa's my lodestar. My friend. My hero.

Introduction

Reading spies and "terrorists"

In 2011, Mullen, a marketing company located in Boston, Massachusetts, developed a series of print and television advertisements featuring the Roomba, a robotic vacuum cleaner, and other affiliated products in a campaign meant to showcase the cutting-edge technology of iRobot. On its website, where one can view all the ads for iRobot, Mullen articulates its approach to "branding" the technology company:

> When iRobot came to us, millions of people owned Roombas, and even more had heard about them. The trouble was, people didn't identify the iRobot brand. So to raise awareness of their brand, we turned iRobot into a verb that was both inclusive and actionable. In a global campaign, we asked the question, "I robot. Do you?" From there, we let the products do the talking. Products like the ever-popular Roomba robotic vacuum to military robots used in Afghanistan showcased this exciting, innovative brand.[1]

One of the television ads featured on Mullen's website presents a range of iRobot products in a montage that starts in a quiet domestic space, arcs out to "public" spaces—including an elementary school classroom, a lab, what can best be described as "urban mean streets," and then to a desert war location, either Iraq or Afghanistan—and closes via a return to a serene interior setting. At each location, an actor says, "iRobot," until the last frame, again set in an appealing interior scene, in which an attractive woman elaborates in accented English, "I robot. Do you?" (Mullen 2011). The cuts between scenes invite the viewer to make connections between the settled, comfortable upper-middle-class bourgeois domesticity so evident in the four opening and one closing frames, on the one hand, and the more "public" frames, which themselves go from "nurturing" places of learning to sites where police and military personnel use violence to ensure "safety," on the other. Just as Mullen's approach emphasizes their intent to turn "iRobot into a verb," this montage stresses how the iRobot products *do something globally*: the Roombas, the learning tools, the SUGV (small unmanned ground vehicles which, according to iRobot's website, "gathe[r] situational awareness in dangerous conditions") all make locations cleaner, better, safer for the people using them (Mullen 2013). The whole created by the montage analogizes housekeeping and military action in the "war on terror," and thus outlines inclusivity in ways that the Mullen team may not have imagined. That is, the iRobots' actions make sites cleaner, better, safer for those of us who "iRobot," which, in this context, becomes a meme transmitted among people who take as a given the inviolate nature of their surroundings.

Robotic vacuum cleaners may seem a long way away from post-9/11 literary representations of spies and "terrorists." Yet, via analyses of American contributions to the popular spy fiction genre and Pakistani fictions featuring the twinned figures of the spy (or his proxy) and the "terrorist," a term frequently conflated with fundamentalist, *Post-9/11 Espionage Fiction in the US and Pakistan* examines the very dynamics that analogize the domestically appealing and the "war on terror," especially as this latter phenomenon takes shape through covert intelligence gathering and overt violence. While in many ways post-9/11 relations between Pakistan and the US appear to rehearse a familiar script, the deterioration of cooperation, the charges of mendacity, and the breaches of sovereignty also force "covert" activities out into the open and publicize them more broadly and immediately. The ubiquity of references to these activities warrants a thorough examination of how we're interpreting them.[2] My argument is that the appropriation by Pakistani writers of various spy fiction conventions insistently tracks how the formulaic and popular nature of post-9/11 American espionage thrillers forwards and reinforces "appropriate" affective responses, often linked to domestic sites and relations, to "terrorism." "Appropriate" in both its adjectival and verb forms crystallizes the work the Pakistani texts do. Beyond "suitable," "appropriate" as an adjective also signifies "belonging to oneself; private; selfish" (*Oxford English Dictionary*) and, thus, endows the affective response promoted by the American texts I examine with a sharply exclusive, even myopic dimension. My use of "appropriate" as a verb undoes these self-centered interests as I mean for the verb to signify the wresting away of genre conventions from exclusive usage in American popular fiction in order to re-place them in different narrative contexts. As the Pakistani texts re-place spy fiction's conventions, they offer another vantage point from which to view the affective appeals common to these conventions' usual deployment in American texts. My argument also contends that the literary intervention into the espionage genre by the Pakistani texts calls attention to without legitimating how the "exceptional" measures taken in both the American and Pakistani fictions inaugurate a social and political order wherein the suspension of laws and morals works to uphold those same laws and morals. The majority of my analyses focus on literary texts, and my hope is that the insights these analyses produce can serve as interpretive interruptions of non-fictive representations of Pakistani–US "war on terror" relations.

My argument involves three interconnected issues: how the events of 11 September 2001 and their aftermath influence new developments in spy fiction as a popular genre, which include the transformation of the spy himself and the emergence of figures who can be taken as the spy's proxy (Chapters 1, 2, and 3); how the appropriation of and experimentation with select elements of this popular genre by Pakistani writers working in English highlights the logic through which the exception, derived from Giorgio Agamben's formulation, becomes the uncontested and even welcomed rule (Chapters 2, 3, and 4); and how analyses of literary narratives concerned with espionage and terrorism can reshape our approach to non-fictive representations of the same concerns (Conclusion). In a sense, my focus on literature makes possible a similarly "literary" reading of representations of the two nations' connections as they emerge in various media and governmental sources. These interconnected issues allow me to develop my broader, overarching argument, outlined above, which begins with the spy's affective appeal and his authoritative role within the genre. Framed in language I use more extensively in the following chapters, the spy acts with a sovereign's power in that he decides who lives and who dies. The recognition of the spy's power, secured in no small measure through his appeal and authority, makes the emergence of his proxy—the private military contractor and the Special Forces Operator (and even the weaponized drone)—all the more significant in that this development also means that these proxies possess the sovereign's power. Further, the expansion of the sovereign's power to include the spy's proxy signals a blurring of the line between the clandestine and the citizens' realms or the creation of an indistinct zone, to echo Agamben again, that colors the sovereign's relation to place, both the place the sovereign protects and the one he subjects to violence. The "terrorist," as one subjected to the sovereign's violence, serves as a figure, I argue, that can introduce a new way of seeing, a new way of reading, a new way of knowing, if we can acknowledge that staid ways of explaining who the "terrorist" is cannot provide a complete encounter with difference.

My analyses will foreground the following Pakistani English-language novels: Mohsin Hamid's novel *The Reluctant Fundamentalist* (2007), Nadeem Aslam's novel *The Wasted Vigil* (2008), Kamila Shamsie's novel *Burnt Shadows* (2009), and H.M. Naqvi's novel *Home Boy* (2009). While far from exhaustive, I'll be drawing on the following American texts to establish the baseline for what I mean by post-9/11 US espionage fiction: David Ignatius's novels *Body of Lies* (2007) and *Blood Money* (2011), Alex Berenson's novel *The Faithful Spy* (2006), Colin MacKinnon's novels *Morning Spy, Evening Spy* (2006) and *The Contractor* (2009), Michael Gruber's novel *The Good Son* (2010), Ben Coes's novel *Coup d'État* (2011), and Dalton Fury's novel *Black Site* (2012).[3] My turn to non-fictive representations of spies and terrorists will concentrate primarily on US media and government representations of that nation's drone program, including the US Department of Justice's leaked White Paper on drone attacks. In Chapters 2, 3, and 4, I deploy a contrapuntal approach wherein I first assess how the Pakistani texts represent the central figure at hand and then use these insights as foils against which I analyze the American texts' representations of the same figure. As I explain below, I use the

Pakistani novels as a brake on the quick-paced, formula-driven American novels so as to engage with the density of these latter texts' familiar and often stereotypical portrayals. Relatedly, that the Pakistani novels are English-language fictions actually proves an asset in the overall intent of this study. That is, I attempt to read post-9/11 American spy fictions *through* Pakistani novels that concern themselves with similar characters, circumstances, and settings. This effort relies on the Pakistani novels being available to an English-speaking and, even more specifically, an American audience. Further, since my analyses don't forward any definitive or exhaustive claims about the spy fiction genre or representations of its stock characters and conventions, I have no stake in any claims of authenticity; indeed, as I discuss below, one of my points is representation's inability to convey fully what difference is. So, I make no argument that these Pakistani fictions amount to *the* Pakistani response to 9/11 and its aftermath, any more than I argue that the American fictions stand in for a single response in the US. Instead, rather than reinforce or debunk a "clash of civilizations" thesis, which itself traffics in essentialisms and authenticities, I devote the following pages to evaluating the implications of literary and non-literary representations of encounters with difference through an examination of the spy, his proxy, and the "terrorist."

As my analyses move between texts by Pakistani and American writers, I implicitly engage with the ongoing conversation about fictive representations of the events of 11 September 2001 and their aftermath in two specific ways: first, my concentration on the appropriation of spy fiction conventions by Pakistani writers signals, as I mention above, a re-placing of this popular genre's formulas, even if the settings are the same, through the generation of representations by non-US writers; and second, I call attention to the breakdown of the previously bifurcated "shadow" world of espionage and the "real" world of citizenship, rights, and democracy to highlight the growing accept-ability of the measures previously covert actions take to provide "security" for those who benefit from the protection of the powerful.[4] The briefest outline of this critical conversation about literary representations of 9/11 involves a chron-ology that starts with a discussion of the inadequacy of language to represent the event itself and/or the hyper-mediatization of the event; it then moves to a focus on trauma; and, most recently, the conversation involves a critique of this traumatic focus accompanied by a call to move beyond a US-centered approach.[5] This last strand necessitates a renewed consideration of both time and place, a need I address with these analyses. As Richard Crownshaw (2011: 758) argues, American post-9/11 literary and cultural responses "are often preoccupied with [...] the time of trauma rather than the space of American territory." Such a preoccupation gets caught up synchronically or cherry picks other iconic moments from American history in order to build a comprehensible narrative around 9/11.[6] Elleke Boehmer (2009) offers a corrective to synchronism in "Postcolonial Writing and Terror," arguing that postcolonial texts move beyond US borders to represent "an alternative mode of seizing hold upon the now" (148) through a restoration of "temporal depth, a sense of the deep layering or thickness of history" (149). To this critical conversation, I add an emphasis on visibility through enacting an interpretive methodology attentive to the "givens" on the surface of mainstream espionage fictions. I use the Pakistani novels, which can't quite be considered exemplars of this popular genre, to offset the recurring and even formulaic representations of the spy, his proxy, and the "terrorist" in the American fictions. These juxtaposed readings allow me to isolate, to examine in slow motion, the density behind these pulp portrayals of current events. Packed within this density, I contend, are worldviews and attitudes—both introduced and reinforced—that normalize and perpetuate a precariousness that envelops us all.[7]

My use of the verb "envelops" indicates the global resonances operating within this study. An expansion beyond US representations of 9/11, which Michael Rothberg (2009: 153) calls a "complementary centrifugal mapping that charts the outward movement of American power," would refuse to rationalize an interiorized gaze for any number of reasons, including those concerned with the Other's purported incomprehensibility (Robbins 2011: 1098), even if this expansion takes place solely through the novel's imaginary. Indeed, Alex Houen (2004: 430) posits the *"potentialist* novel" as a viable way to explore how "the novel's other world of possibility might present an effective engagement with the world, [while] at the same time being [...] experientially affective." My own arguments regarding spy fiction's affective appeal follow up on Houen's speculation over the affective resonance of the *"potentialist* novel" by examining how the intervention spurred by the Pakistani texts links these appeals to broader political dynamics. Further, my "contrapuntal reading" of the Pakistani fictions, to borrow (and inflect) Edward Said's phrase,[8] centers these texts, giving flesh to the "spectral elusiveness" haunting not only American espionage fiction but also, according to Timothy Marr (2006: 522), all hemispheric American literatures. Referring to both pre- and post-9/11 eras, Marr's project is to latitudinalize the already longitudinalized field of American Studies by exploring how, for centuries, writers in the western hemisphere "have evoked [...] Islamic difference to imagine a variety of *unincorporated spaces* that lie beyond the full control of continental systems of cultural power" (Marr 2006: 522, emphasis added). Where Marr metaphorizes Islamic difference as a conceptual space of the unassimilable in American literature, I examine how the texts I've chosen use the threat of terrorism to configure places and, thus, position or incorporate Muslim and non-Muslim presences in relation to one another.

By using terrorism as a critical pivot point, I align my project with Boehmer's description of postcolonialism as a "resistance to empire and its post-imperial aftermath [which] unnervingly to some, [...] aligns more closely with some of the theories and significations of *terror* (as in anti-colonial violence, for example), than it does with *globalization*," a term which frequently manifests itself literarily as hybridity, transnationalism, or other discourses of merging and connection (Boehmer 2009: 143). That is, in all my selected texts, I deliberately read for (and not from) the vilified and villainized perspective, which espionage fiction's penchant for binaristic terms makes easy, to assess the terms that frame such a perspective. The representations' contemporaneousness broadens each individual text and, again given generic predilections, does so without the reassurances of intercultural harmony or cooperation that characterize Boehmer's figuration of globalization. To be bereft of these reassurances is not to posit or reinforce a "clash of civilization" theory, however. In place of the certainties a "clash" theory offers, my analyses pose additional questions about how representations of spies and "terrorists" shape our affective responses and our political tolerances.

I form these questions through a surface-level interpretive methodology, which strikes me as particularly germane to a post-9/11 context. Martin Randall (2011) identifies "a central trope of representation that so many of the artists and writers who have created work dealing with 9/11 have struggled with—namely the tensions between what is 'seen' and 'not seen'" (5). In making this identification, Randall specifically focuses on the 102 minutes between the first plane hitting the North Tower of the World Trade Center and the collapse of both towers, and all the events that occurred in between. Retrospectively, of course, artists, writers, politicians, nearly everyone imposes a narrative linking these events. At the time the events happened, however, we had no framing devices other than those provided by the cameras capturing the images. This knowing/not knowing represents the tension to which Randall refers. Even as artists and writers have struggled with this tension, especially in terms of the inadequacy of representation, many texts, I argue, paradoxically hide the visible, with all its attendant fears, anxieties, inequalities, and brutalities, by normalizing it, as does the iRobot commercial I mentioned at the top of this introduction. In other words, representations sit within narratives whose parameters permit only a limited acknowledgment of the material consequences that follow from what the narrative says the event—here, 9/11—means. Even if all narratives work in this way, the task of seeing the unsee-able, of tracing those consequences, remains urgent in the sense that the task may also encourage the recognition of the Other in terms that value her/his humanity and complexity. Such an opening outward stands as a necessary corrective to the navel-gazing often accompanying narratives, the recursiveness of which frequently reinforces the centrality of our selves.

My central argument is that the Pakistani texts track how spy fiction acknowledges the "appropriate" affective responses to "terrorism," and that, at the same time, they call attention to the "exceptional" measures the genre deploys to normalize the suspension of laws and morals in the name of those laws and morals. I've reached these conclusions via an interpretive methodology that pivots on a visible/invisible metaphor. The pivot between visibility and invisibility refers to how the ordinary or the visible appears so straightforward that we don't even see what's in front of us: post-9/11 spy fiction, for instance, visualizes the "terrorist" in a way that marks a "difference" explicitly but, in doing so, also crowds out more complex approaches to difference. The ordinary renders these more complex approaches to difference invisible by offering an explanation for the "difference" it portrays. My interest is in examining the power of these explanations rather than to accept them as full claims to knowing the Other. In effect, *Post-9/11 Espionage Fiction* is an attempt to think about how specific types of literature represent the "difference" of the Muslim Other and to explore how these representations carry over into non-fictive realms. Broadly, my approach borrows in part from both Object-Oriented Ontology and Speculative Realism, on the one hand, and relational ontology, which is more common to literary studies, on the other. Jane Bennett (2012: 227) describes an object-oriented approach as an effort "to make both objects and relations the periodic focus of theoretical attention," which I attempt to do here by reading post-9/11 American spy fictions alongside Pakistani novels that draw upon many of the same figures, tropes, and conventions. My readings are thus both across fictions and within specific texts. Furthermore, given the international scope of my reading, Graham Harman's theorizing about how Speculative Realism may "translate" into literary studies provides me with an entry point into thinking about a treatment of difference that exists outside the play of signifiers. Harman (2012: 196) explains how Speculative Realism "views objects or things as genuine realities deeper than any of the relations in which they become involved." Contexts and the representations that comprise them can't fully explain an object or a thing or, for my purposes, difference. Very specifically, Harman emphasizes how this conviction regarding the realness of objects prevents their translation into "masterable knowledge" (196). Importantly, Harman insists that Speculative Realism doesn't posit as possible "direct access to the world" (197–98), but, rather, insists on how the text "runs deeper than any coherent meaning" (200). Speaking of literary texts specifically, Harman claims that Speculative Realism shows how texts "*cannot be fully identified with* [their] *surroundings*" (202, emphasis in original), which I take to mean any context in which we would place these texts. Such an inability to identify texts fully with their surroundings becomes more evident, I think, as I line up the Pakistani and American novels side by side. The relations I create between these novels help illustrate how none of the texts completely enclose meaning. Further, with respect to difference, Harman's caution against full identification or mastery underscores, again, the "realness" of difference beyond its representation. To my mind, Harman's interest in deflecting claims of mastery relies upon an idea of excessiveness, of uncontainability. Difference, then, becomes an "object," so to speak, that cannot be fully apprehended through representation; difference exceeds our ability to make it visible. This ability to exceed the visible is, in my view, precisely why we need to examine what we do see, especially when what is presented, what's represented, announces itself as a claim to full knowing.

My interest in retaining what Bennett calls a relational ontology in my approach prompts me to articulate more precisely how context figures in my analyses. As I've suggested at several points already, the temporal simultaneity (of production, of publication) of my selected texts contributes to a primary context. Given my earlier reference to Boehmer, I don't mean for this adjacency to be a call for synchronism; rather, I see the texts as assembling a fuller (but not completely full) picture of how post-9/11 fiction represents spies and "terrorists." Thus, despite Harman's rejection of the term, I adopt the notion of "assemblage" as a necessary component of my analyses. With a slight alteration, Harman's (2012: 202) question regarding culture's influence on literature—"[W]hy [are] *certain* things [...] connected rather than others?"— accounts for this adoption. In other words, I treat the sum total of my texts as an echo chamber wherein I can discern (dis)similarities in their representations of difference, which reverses in the Pakistani texts wherein the non-Muslims and/or the Americans are the Others, and can speculate over how these (dis)similarities function. Prompted by the visible and invisible, I adopt a "shallow" interpretive methodology that tries to account for how the visible makes difference invisible as it forwards "difference" as if this latter is plain as day. At the same time, I also avoid claims to full knowing so as to acknowledge the "realness" of difference beyond my own acts of interpretation.

In an effort to contextualize my surface-level methodology, I first want to outline how it differs from an interpretive methodology that's been dominant in literary studies for more than a few decades. There are a variety of ways to refer to an interpretive methodology premised on a depth metaphor—that is, an approach that seeks to uncover what a text can't or won't say. Following Paul Ricoeur (1977), we could call it a "hermeneutic of suspicion"; like Eve Sedgwick (1997), we could adopt "paranoid reading"; for Bruno Latour (2004), it's "conspiratorial"; Heather Love (2010) likes "deep reading"; or, we could tip our hat to Althusser and opt for the tried, true, and familiar phrase beloved of Marxists the world over: "symptomatic reading." For those partial to psychoanalysis, I suppose this is just another way of saying "psychoanalysis." Any which way, this methodology functions, according to Sedgwick (1997), as a "strong theory," posited with too little critical consideration as *the* way to make meaning.

Morrison's *Playing in the Dark* (1992), like Edward Said's treatment of Jane Austen's *Mansfield Park* in *Culture and Imperialism* (1993) or Gayatri Spivak's reading of *Jane Eyre* in "Three Women's Texts and a Critique of Imperialism" (1985), represents the best work, in my opinion, that "deep reading" can produce. In other words, a "hermeneutic of suspicion" can constructively call attention to the disenfranchised and oppressed. Such a methodology has done and will continue to do important work. One of the reasons that Morrison's and Said's contributions are so valuable is that they recognize how reading, interpretation, and literary analysis are learned and situated activities, just as is the production of texts. In *The World, the Text, and the Critic*, for instance, Said asserts:

> The point is that texts have ways of existing that even in their most rarefied form are always enmeshed in circumstance, time, place, and society—in short, they are in the world, and hence worldly. Whether a text is

preserved or put aside for a period, whether it is on a library shelf or not, whether it is considered dangerous or not: these matters have to do with a text's being in the world, which is a more complicated matter than the private process of reading. The same implications are undoubtedly true of critics in their capacities as readers and writers in the world.

(Said 1983: 135)

As texts make "worlds" through the processes of production and interpretation, their representations are never "neutral or innocent," to cite another of Said's (1983: 241) claims. We gain a fuller understanding of how our engagement with texts creates meaning as we locate them and ourselves in the complex fields of pasts and presents. Often enough, this locating activity does involve the critic in an "excavation" of sorts, but such digging need not preclude the dedication of a similar diligence to what exists on the text's "surface."

Not all deployments of "symptomatic reading" appear quite so attentive to this situatedness, though, which leaves me wondering what's at stake in continuing to conduct such readings or in trying to widen our critical scope to include alternative methodologies. My disquiet over the hegemony of "symptomatic reading" emerges in part from how it functions tautologically. Eve Sedgwick (1997) argues, for example, that this method's emphasis on "uncovering the hidden" "can't help or can't stop or can't do anything other than proving the very same assumptions with which it began" (13). Such interpretive techniques are, in Bruno Latour's (2004) words, "rather poor trick[s]" (241) which "tur[n] those [objects of belief] into fetishes that are supposed to be nothing but mere empty white screens on which is projected the power of society, domination, whatever," all the while allowing critics to treat their own theories as "indisputable facts" (238). Latour's claim of indisputability hints at the position that the critic who deploys this methodology occupies. With no small measure of snark, Latour congratulates his fellow critics:

> You [the critic] are always right! When naïve believers are clinging forcefully to their objects, claiming that they are made to do things because of their gods, their poetry, their cherished objects, you can turn all of those attachments into so many fetishes and humiliate all the believers by showing that it is nothing but their own project, that you, yes you alone, can see.
>
> (Latour 2004: 239)

Such certitude proves a heady elixir, as Edward Said notes, when he asserts the transfixing properties of "strong theories" whose very ubiquity and uncritical deployment lands critics in "ideological trap[s]" (Said 1983: 241).

Beyond what may appear this petty portrait of the practitioner of a "hermeneutic of suspicion" (or this portrait of the petty practitioner), we can detect some vexing ramifications. In Said's (1983: 245) critique of Foucault and his adherents (among whom he once counted himself), Said worries that falling under the thrall of a "strong theory" risks "justify[ing] political quietism with sophisticated intellectualism, at the same time wishing to appear realistic, in touch with the world of power and reality, as well as historical and antiformalistic in [...] bias." Even more than where "paranoid reading" places the critic, this risk of quietism is what concerns me most, for, in my view, one of the foremost goals of any critical activity is to specify how culture as a "realm" enjoins its participants/consumers to specific attachments that can have very material consequences. With respect to my topic—framing the "terrorist"—I wonder about the "willed" blindness attending these attachments.

My own attempts to carry out this critical objective employ "shallow reading," which I adapt from Heather Love's notion of "surface reading" or a methodology that "considers what texts do say, rather than what they don't or can't" (Love 2010: 383), and which is derived, in part, from Stephen Best and Sharon Marcus's definition of "surface": that which "insists on being looked *at* rather than what we must train ourselves to see *through*" (Best and Marcus 2009: 9). I hope to illustrate through a series of examples what this method looks like and why I find its use a matter of urgency in the context of post-9/11 representations of the spy, his proxy, and the "terrorist."

An urgent example: drones as instruments used to carry out targeted killings, a topic I return to in Chapter 3 and the Conclusion. Scott Shane's "Debating a Court to Vet Drone Strikes," appearing in *The New York Times*, focused on the lack of transparency in the drone strike decision-making process and laid out congressional concern over the inordinate amount of power the executive branch has had in making these decisions. The creation of a "drone court," an option supported by a subsequent *Times* editorial, represents one possible way to institute some checks and balances. Outlining the issue, Shane's article states:

> Even if they are glad Mr. Awlaki [an American citizen targeted in a September 2011 drone attack] is dead, many Americans are uneasy that a president can use secret evidence to label a citizen a terrorist and order his execution without a trial or judge's ruling. Hence the idea of court oversight for targeted killing, which on Thursday [February 2013], unexpectedly, got serious discussion from senators and Mr. Brennan [Obama's nominee for CIA Director].
>
> (Shane 2013a)

In effect, the proposed court would bring to light how and why intelligence agencies target suspects. The article I've just cited also states that this new court may only consider whether American citizens can be added to a targeted kill list (Shane 2013a).[9] Significantly, while the creation of a "drone court" may provide the appearance of oversight or checks and balances, it really doesn't alter public awareness of the use of drone strikes. That is, a court may provide details, if such information isn't classified, but the American public—indeed the international public—has known for years about this targeted killing practice. In a metaphorical sense for those who reside in the US and literally for those who live in places where these drone strikes take place, then, knowledge of these killings has been right in front of our faces.

The letters to the editor this article on the "drone court" elicited highlight some of the ways we might process the overt nature of the drone attacks and targeted killings. Bishop Desmond Tutu writes the first letter *The New York Times* choose to publish. Bishop Tutu objects most strenuously to the possibility that a "drone court" would hear only cases pertaining to American citizens. Such legalistic discrimination prompts Tutu to wonder:

> Do the United States and its people really want to tell those of us who live in the rest of the world that our lives are not of the same value as yours? That President Obama can sign off on a decision to kill us with less worry about judicial scrutiny than if the target is an American? Would your Supreme Court really want to tell humankind that we, like the slave Dred Scott in the 19th century, are not as human as you are? I cannot believe it.
>
> (*The New York Times* 2013)

Tutu's vision of a scaled humanity occasions a troubling analogy wherein the Nobel Laureate likens the US's response to Osama bin Laden and his followers with apartheid; both historical phenomena, Tutu claims, "undermine your moral standards and your humanity" (*The New York Times* 2013). Provocatively, the *Times* included a second letter on the same topic, one written by a Harvey Karron from Coram, NY. Karron frames the drone attacks as imperative, a more than acceptable response to an individual's decision "to cross over to the enemy's side[, thereby relinquishing] his or her right to be protected by the United States government" (ibid.). In Karron's estimation, not to kill these people would be "irresponsible" (ibid.). These two letters' appearance in the *Times*—first Tutu's and then Karron's—creates a conversational effect. Not only are they both obviously responses to Shane's article, but, by way of their appearance, they also exist in a conversation with each other. Taken together, we can see a slippage between "human" and "American": clearly, Tutu views the category "human" as more all encompassing, but Karron implicitly supports a separation, as he recognizes "rights" as attending to national and not human identities. The fulcrum between these two positions aligns with Giorgio Agamben's (1995) interrelated notions of the state of exception and *homo sacer*, as Tutu's and Karron's views both hinge upon sovereign power over "bare life," a discussion I develop in the following chapters. In brief, then, these two letters acknowledge what has been explicit since the start of these drone campaigns, and, with Tutu's admonition in mind, these letters begin to show what I mean by how the visible renders difference invisible in order to make explicit a "difference" that can be known, contained, and conquered.

Outline of the book

Chapter 1, "Genre," explores the book's first issue: how the events of 11 September 2001 and their aftermath influence new developments in spy fiction as a popular genre. After a brief overview of espionage fiction's origins and critical reception, this chapter focuses on these developments. To understand their significance, I metaphorize the concept of "propaganda by deed," which stands in as a shorthand for the shallow reading methodology I've discussed here, to account for how the Pakistani fictions I analyze draw attention to how representations of terrorism and attendant concepts and figures are always already metafictional. I also explore spy fiction's conventions, with a particular focus on readerly identification with the spy (or his proxy), to promote an understanding of how these stock-in-trade elements shape interpretive practices and knowledge claims. Together, my metaphorization of "propaganda by deed" and the identification of conventions anticipates in more precise terms the intervention the post-9/11 Pakistani novels undertake—an intervention I will lay out in the following chapters.

Chapter 2, "Spy," develops at greater length the preliminary considerations of the spy's affective appeal laid out in Chapter 1. In doing so, this chapter's interest in the figure of the spy in both the American and Pakistani fictions addresses the overlap between two of the book's main issues: new developments in the genre and the appropriation of select generic elements by Pakistani writers. In this chapter, Nadeem Aslam's *The Wasted Vigil* allows for the critical tracing of two processes: identification and revelation. Identification comes about through the affective appeals issued by representations of the American spy and encourages readers to connect with this figure. The spy's relate-ability matters, not least because it directs attention to this figure's own affective attachments and away from the historical and political circumstances giving rise to the plot itself. Through such connections, the spy gains credibility and trust, cementing his ability to reveal the "truth" of the novel's contexts and to claim mastery over the Other. By securing readerly investment in the figure of the spy, a dynamic brought to light in Aslam's novel and played out repeatedly in the American texts, spy fiction makes more acceptable the spy's actions and his relation to place and the Others who inhabit it.

Similar to Chapter 2, Chapter 3, "Proxy," also addresses the overlap between generic developments and appropriations by elaborating upon a point raised in Chapter 1: the emergence of the spy's proxy in the figures of the private military contractor and the Special Forces Operator. The analyses in this chapter start with Kamila Shamsie's *Burnt Shadows* and then turn to an array of American texts to build upon the argument laid out in Chapter 2 regarding the ahistoricizing impulses at work in explanations for terrorism that rely on what Mahmood Mamdani (2004) calls "Culture Talk," a discourse structured according to essentializing hierarchies. The introduction of the military contractor and the Special Forces Operator into post-9/11 spy fiction, which occurs in texts by both American and Pakistani writers, matters because it marks the entrance of non-spies into espionage's traditionally closed and covert arenas. Rather than morph the contractor or the Special Forces Operator into a clandestine figure, however, I argue that this entrance remakes the arena of espionage into an open, overt site wherein the suspension of laws and morals becomes the norm or, in other words, wherein the exception becomes the usual state of being. Borrowing heavily from Agamben's formulation of the state of exception, this chapter contends that the proxy's entrance onto the scene makes visible and normalizes the state of exception.

Chapter 4, "Terrorist," focuses on the "seen" and the "said" of the US Department of Homeland Security's "If You See Something, Say Something™" campaign, in order to examine how post-9/11 Pakistani and US fictions represent the figure of the "terrorist." This focus allows me to develop one of the interconnected issues I identified in the Introduction: namely, how the Pakistani appropriation of spy fiction's conventions highlights the logic through which the state of exception becomes acceptable. I use the ambivalence that two Pakistani novels employ to portray the suspected "terrorist" to call into question the "knowledge" about "terrorists" produced by the explanations offered in the US fictions. Framed in the Department of Homeland Security's campaign, my analyses concentrate, first, on the "seen." H.M. Naqvi's *Home Boy* and Mohsin Hamid's *The Reluctant Fundamentalist* both complicate the channeling of sanctioned violence toward racially marked subjects by foregrounding how the "terrorist's" body—which is "seen"— stands in relation to the law. In doing so, these Pakistani fictions individuate without psychologizing and, thus, encourage a recognition of circumstance rather than abstraction or universalization. The "said" provides the framework for the second part of my analyses, which take as their subject the American fictions. With the ambivalence featured in the Pakistani novels in mind, I contrast the certainty with which the American fictions "know" the "terrorist." Of particular interest here is how these explanations make use of tropes derived from "Culture Talk" and how these tropes then justify the relegation of the "terrorist" to the state of exception.

"Conclusion: Drones" addresses my final major issue: how an examination of literary narratives concerned with espionage and terrorism can reshape our approach to non-fictive representations of the same concerns. My aim is to explore what is gained when shallow reading as an interpretive approach— honed throughout the preceding chapters via the metaphorization of the Pakistani novels as instances of "propaganda by deed"—takes as its object not only genre fiction but also newspaper and magazine articles, and even government reports dealing with the US government's ongoing drone program. Rather than privilege the non-fictive texts as more "real" than the fictive ones, my point is to identify where phenomena such as affective appeals, "Culture Talk," the sovereign ban, and *homo sacer*—all addressed in my literary analyses—jump genre. The coincidence of these phenomena's appearance, then, within both fictive and non-fictive representations, made visible precisely through the contrapuntal reading of the Pakistani novels' appropriations of espionage conventions, promotes a more "literate"—but, perhaps, no less contentious—understanding of the Other.

Notes

1 See all of Mullen's iRobot work here: www.mullen.com/client/irobot/.
2 I want to emphasize that, while in the US we are aware of the American government's activities, such as rendition and drone attacks, we don't have many details. In other words, we have the references, but we don't have specifics, which the government protects under the heading of "national security."
3 My selection criteria for the post-9/11 American fictions include: all the novels need to address 9/11 in some way; they need to include Pakistan as a setting or Pakistanis as characters; and they need to involve covert activity even if the American protagonist isn't a spy proper—that is, he could be a contractor or a Special Forces Operator who works with the Central Intelligence Agency (CIA) or other US intelligence agency, or he could be a pawn in a larger covert operation. Only Ignatius's *Blood Money* and Gruber's *The Good Son* feature females as central parts of covert operations; all other female characters are accessories to the male agents and operators.
4 I delve more specifically into how all of my selected post-9/11 spy fictions contribute to a reconsideration of that popular genre in Chapter 1.
5 Ann Keniston and Jeanne Follansbee Quinn's (2009) "Introduction," as well as Alex Houen's (2004) "Novel Spaces," provide a concise overview of these first two points. Richard Crownshaw (2011) acknowledges and attempts to extend the trauma trope. Richard Gray (2011), Michael Rothberg (2009), Bimbisar Irom (2012), and Bruce Robbins (2011) all issue the call for moving beyond the US. More recently, Catherine Morley (2011) intervenes in Gray's and Rothberg's arguments, warning against their prescriptiveness, by re-reading some of the primary sources the latter two critics view as too provincial. Similarly, Ahmed Gamal (2012) attempts to recuperate some of the novels, including John Updike's *Terrorist* and Don DeLillo's *Falling Man*, from charges levied by Gray *et al.* See also my *Contemporary Pakistani Fiction in English*, especially Chapter 7.
6 One obvious example of this cherry picking: the resonance between the flag-raising photos at Ground Zero and Iwo Jima. See Gary Westwall's (2008) "One Image Begets Another."
7 I mean to echo only in part Judith Butler's (2004) discussion of precariousness in *Precarious Life*. As Butler does, I acknowledge:

> that both our political and ethical responsibilities are rooted in the recognition that radical forms of self-sufficiency and unbridled sovereignty are, by definition, disrupted by the larger global processes of which they are a part, that no final control can be secured, and that final control is not, cannot be, an ultimate value.
>
> (xiii)

At the same time, I find convincing Sunera Thobani's (2007: 176) critique of Butler's work on 9/11 for its invocation of victim's discourse and its tendency to universalize loss in terms of the violence done to white subjectivity. I discuss the prominence of victim's discourse in post-9/11 American spy fiction in Chapter 2.
8 In *Culture and Imperialism*, Said (1993: 67) asserts, "In reading a text, one must open it out both to what went into it and to what its author excluded. Each cultural work is a vision of a moment, and we must juxtapose that vision with the various

revisions it later provoked [...]" The texts I examine here have a simultaneity, a temporal and geographical proximity, that prompts me to inflect Said's concept with a different emphasis. Where Said advises readers to consider both inclusions and exclusions, with the latter made all the more evident via the text's historical accumulations, I juxtapose contemporaneous Pakistani and American texts in an attempt to discern (dis)similar emphases and elisions.

9 Shane's (2013a) article also calls attention to the fact that most recent targets of these drone attacks have been "a mixed bag of midlevel militants and foot soldiers whose focus is often more on the Pakistani or Yemeni authorities than on the United States." The status of these targets stands in some tension to the US government's claims that the drone program targets only high-level suspects.

1   Genre

Well over one hundred years before 9/11, European anarchists proposed the concept of "propaganda by deed" as a way to refer to acts that we can now identify as precursors to contemporary terrorism. "Propaganda by deed," as these anarchists initially conceived of it, emphasized the symbolic power of action over idea as the most effective way to convey revolutionary ideals to large numbers of people, many of whom were illiterate peasants and laborers, at the same time. The coinage of this phrase, coinciding roughly as it did with the advanced mechanization of print media and the emergence of spy fiction as a popular genre in the late nineteenth century, provides this chapter with its foundational concept. More specifically, "propaganda by deed" relies on an attempt to control somewhat tightly the interpretive relationship between actor-event-audience, thus automatically necessitating a readerly practice attentive to the explicit. Such a reading practice aligns to some degree with the argument for shallow reading I laid out in the Introduction in that both focus on what the text says, the violence it presents, rather than primarily excavating a hidden or silenced meaning. Here, I metaphorize the already figurative concept of "propaganda by deed" to theorize how the Pakistani appropriation of spy fiction's conventions both highlights a cross-cultural "illiteracy" and instructs—without prescribing—readers on how to re-read the post-9/11 American espionage novels for precisely these conventions and their role in the explicit portrayal of violence. "Propaganda by deed" thus becomes, in my usage, a way of conceptualizing the post-9/11 Pakistani novels' intervention into the espionage genre, especially in terms of this genre's representation of American and Pakistani relations. In the next three chapters, I construct this intervention, first, by analyzing one or more of the Pakistani fictions to see how they portray the figure at hand—the spy, his proxy, or the "terrorist"—and then I use that portrayal as foil against which I assess the US fictions' portrayals of the same figure. The object of all my analyses is to identify "illiteracies" and ways to read through them, always using the Pakistani texts as primers in this regard.[1] My efforts to develop further my notion of shallow reading through the metaphorization of "propaganda by deed" and, as I discuss below, a contrapuntal approach to the texts themselves allow me to address the first interconnected issue I identified in the Introduction: namely, how post-9/11 Pakistani and US spy fictions manifest new developments in spy fiction as a popular genre.

In what follows, I first demonstrate how and why I read "propaganda by deed" as a metaphor for the Pakistani fictions' efforts at targeted communication that exceeds the constraints of convention. Then, I consider how an examination of these conventions also demands attention to the genre's historical locatedness. These contextual concerns matter, because they help situate how the genre, as a popular cultural form, relates to and represents (or doesn't) ideology and politics. From there, I explore spy fiction's conventions, with a particular focus on readerly identification with the spy (or his proxy), to promote an understanding of how these stock-in-trade elements shape interpretive practices and knowledge claims. The identification of conventions also helps anticipate in more precise terms the intervention the post-9/11 Pakistani novels undertake—an intervention I will lay out in the following chapters.

While not all critics and commentators focused on 9/11 connect the events of that day to earlier terrorist acts made possible by technological innovations—specifically, the "propaganda by deed" anarchist violence of the 1880s and 1890s facilitated by the invention of dynamite in 1866 (Cole 2009: 301)—most do acknowledge terrorist acts as forms of communication or, even more specifically, as propaganda.[2] Maura Conway (2004: 21) sees the connection as so fundamental "that without communication there can be no terrorism." Maurice Tugwell (1986: 5) goes a step further by classifying terrorism as a communicative subset of propaganda: "they [terrorism and propaganda] both seek to influence a mass audience in a way that is intended to benefit the sponsor."[3] With respect to 9/11 specifically, Mark Sedgwick makes an explicit link between al-Qaeda and the nineteenth-century European anarchists who coined the phrase "propaganda by deed," interpreting each group's actions in terms of the shared conviction that terrorism possesses vast communicative power rather than in terms of religion (Sedgwick 2004: 795). Defining terrorism as a communicative and/or propagandistic act facilitates analyses focused on the construction and interpretation of representations rather than on assumptions of primordial identities or cultures.

Such analyses focus on many of the same elements as rhetorical and discursive investigations. For instance, Tugwell's use of the terms "influence" and "sponsor" calls forth the commonalities terrorist events share, no matter their specific historical circumstances: sender, message, and audience.[4] Note that "victim" does not appear on this list, and its paradoxical absence only serves to underscore the idea, howsoever cold it may appear, that terrorist acts also function as types of representation. The focus, then, is on how the event comes to make meaning. As Kenneth Payne (2009: 110) explains, "The propagandist is a storyteller, who must craft credible and compelling narratives for his audience," thus making propaganda "a conscious act of construction." Within this framework of intentionality, the propagandist's/terrorist's success hinges not just on the violence of the act itself but also on how "well" or "accurately" the audience(s) read(s) that violence. Thus, representations of these acts then add another communicative or interpretive layer on top of the act itself. Arguably, just as the propagandist/terrorist engages in "a conscious act of construction," those actors producing representations of terrorist events surely must also construct their stories with some degree of awareness. Without chasing after vast media or governmental conspiracies, the germane point here, as Jeffory Clymer (2003: 20) asserts, is "to determine how certain acts become implicated in various plots, scenarios, and narratives that are woven both *before* an incident and in its aftermath." Clymer's interest in emplotment serves as a reminder that the representation of extra-fictional events follows conventions, which themselves set and elicit specific readerly expectations, just as fictional events do. With respect to my purpose, this acknowledgment of the construction of meaning surrounding terrorism—that is, the idea of terrorism and reports of terrorism as representations of representations— highlights what's to be gained by reading the Pakistani fictions alongside the US ones: in doing so, we call attention to the many layers of interpretation operating as convention turns to formula in popular genres like espionage fiction and, in turn, what reading of these layers the fictions themselves encourage.

Before delving into how fictions deepen these insights into the extra-fictional relationship between terrorism and propaganda, though, I want to trace the specific lineaments of "propaganda by deed," that historical concept coined by European anarchists in the 1870s.[5] Even more specifically, according to Alex Houen (1998: 995), "propaganda by deed" was "officially introduced in 1876 at the Anarchist International to inaugurate a policy of political violence that would assert a radical materiality [...]" The concept's emphasis on materiality locates it within a specific historical moment in more than one way. First, the material conditions that gave rise to "propaganda by deed" include markers of "progress," such as Alfred Nobel's 1866 invention of dynamite (Cole 2009: 301) and the development of a "mass press during the same era" (Clymer 2003: 7). Dynamite's heretofore unprecedented destructive potency contributes to the concept's development in a clear way. The press's role is as necessary, for the anarchists' deeds required that added layer of representation, as well as that representation's distribution, to accumulate meaning. Clymer describes the relationship between the anarchists and the mass press as nearly symbiotic:

> Newspapers' dependence on the regularly occurring disruptions of the norm that count as "news" seems ready-made for terrorist incidents, which is of course one reason that modern terrorism and the mass press came to maturity together in the decades around the turn of the century.
> (Clymer 2003: 9)

In this relationship, the newspapers (and other communication technologies, such as the telegraph) blur the line between information and sensationalism in their coverage of terrorist acts, for, effectively, they "provid[ed] a free and fast external communication network for the terrorists" (Schmid and de Graaf 1982: 13). Somewhat ironically, the anarchists need the mass media publicity machine even as their politics position them against the monied interests controlling these outlets. As Alex Schmid and Janny de Graaf assert, the ownership of the newspaper industry by nineteenth-century "press barons" "had in practice all but destroyed the equality of freedom of speech. [...] The dynamite the anarchists used served, in a sense, to overthunder the noise of the rotary press" (Schmid and de Graaf 1982: 10–11). Thus, one way "propaganda by deed" as a concept speaks to specific material developments in the late nineteenth century is through its connections with both explosive and print technologies.

A second way the concept bears material concerns is via the anarchists' intended audience. Historical materialism informed European anarchist ideology in the late nineteenth century. According to David Miller, anarchists devised "propaganda by deed," because they thought:

> that the masses [were] generally impervious to ordinary forms of written and verbal propaganda but [could] be aroused by forms of direct action against the state and against capitalist property that [would take] place before their eyes.
>
> (Miller 1984: 99)

Cast as immune or indifferent to conventional forms of communication, the "masses," the anarchists figured, would both understand and respond to sensational actions. These tired laborers—urban and rural dwelling alike—"had no inclination to spend their evenings reading socialist literature" (Miller 1984: 99), if they could read at all, that is. For, as Conway (2004: 21) points out, "High levels of illiteracy in nineteenth-century Europe imposed serious limitations on conventional text-based propaganda."[6] For anarchists, then, "propaganda by deed" helped them combat both a figurative and a literal illiteracy. To whatever degree the "masses" were indifferent to the anarchists' socialist message, these laborers could not "read" their "real" relations to the means of production. Of course, for those laborers who could not actually read, the anarchists' strategy would also educate them on their "real" relations, too. The actions labeled "propaganda by deed" were thus primers on how to understand reality "properly."

With this didactic purpose in mind, the message conveyed by these terrorist deeds needs to be readily apparent. "Propaganda by deed" depends upon a communications loop wherein the terrorists' intention comes through clearly in the act, and, as I note above, the audiences matter more in this paradigm than do the actual victims. Schmid and de Graaf (1982: 15) break down this communicative chain by identifying "a sender, the terrorist, a message generator, the victim, and a receiver, the enemy and/or the public." By labeling the victim a "message generator," this scheme illustrates the figurative power lurking within "propaganda by deed." Further, Schmid and de Graaf's "and/ or" formulation highlights the deed's intended multiple audiences. Mark Sedgwick (2004: 803) sees the possibility of reaching the "potential opponents of the group attacked," who would presumably be a part of Schmid and de Graaf's "public," as the most important element of terrorism's communicative chain. Despite this emphasis on the terrorists' intention, though, the immediacy or transparency of signification presumed by "propaganda by deed" is untenable. Calling such a presumption a "deman[d for] an unlikely cohesion," Sarah Cole (2009: 307) insists upon the relatively uncontainable openness of communicative chains or, simply, interpretation. Part of the messiness Cole suggests with her suspicious view of cohesion resides in the possibility of the deed's multiple (un)intended audiences interpreting the act in unintended ways. Just as suspicious, Clymer (2003: 17) speculates that, "if terrorism is a form of violence that operates on a linguistic model [i.e. "propaganda by deed"], acts will always reach multiple audiences whose attitudes, sympathies, and political orientations will diverge significantly." For all the anarchists' and terrorists' interest in controlling the messages conveyed by their deeds, the figurative basis for "propaganda by deed" holds within itself the potential to escape that control.

The excessive or spectacular nature of "propaganda by deed" compounds this notion of escaping control. As a concept with a lot of bang, "propaganda by deed," by definition, constitutes "wildly excessive" communication (Cole 2009: 307). For Alex Houen (2002: 2, emphasis in original), the events labeled as such "could only be experienced and expressed as *hyperbole*." Houen's adverbial qualification—"only"—suggests an inadequacy in the face of the deed's excessiveness, as if the deed itself stretches the ability to represent, a point that echoes my discussion of the representation of "difference"/difference in the Introduction. Thus, even if the perpetrators were able to convey their message transparently, the hyperbolic aspects of "propaganda by deed" ensure that their efforts would fall short: any codes available to talk about or try to represent the event *as it happens* or *after the fact* lack the power to capture the deed's meaning definitively. The oft-repeated claims that what happened in Manhattan on 11 September 2001 seemed like those over-the-top Hollywood blockbusters makes this point: people had no adequate form of representation other than this filmic analogy, but, at the same time, they were aware of the analogy's poverty. This representational insufficiency calls to mind once again Clymer's interest in emplotment, as the narratives audiences use to represent, howsoever inadequately, the terrorist deeds amount to attempts to control meaning. In this way, such narratives illustrate as much about that audience's values, biases, and (conceptual, political, ideological) limitations as they do the terrorists'.

This excessiveness and the efforts to control it connect back to the illiteracy "propaganda by deed" was supposed to surmount. The motivating power of illiteracy understood both literally and figuratively emphasizes the communicative strength of "propaganda by deed" without necessarily accounting for how problematic this attribution of strength is. For my purposes, though, this motivating illiteracy stands in for the divides in our post-9/11 era—real and perceived—between "us" and "them." "Propaganda by deed" as I (re-)frame it here denotes the Pakistani texts' engagement with the American ones through the former's appropriation of spy fiction's conventions, and, I argue, one of the resulting dynamics involves how these Pakistani texts broach this illiteracy by challenging the narratives and tropes the American texts perpetuate. More generally, I contend that "propaganda by deed"—the representation of representation I mention above—presents an opportunity to view literature about terrorism as a self-conscious act.[7] Following this line of thinking, literary depictions of terrorism provide readers with a unique vantage point on the layered representations operating extra-fictionally. Such is precisely the point Margaret Scanlan makes in her *Plotting Terror* (2001), a study that examines the affinity fictionalized writers have for terrorists. Scanlan argues that these fictionalizations "elucidate the process that allows militants, journalists, and politicians to construct terrorism as a political reality" (2). In short, the analysis of literary representations of terrorism can help us understand extra-literary representations, too. By adopting "propaganda by deed" as a metaphor for the Pakistani texts' appropriation of spy fiction's conventions and themes, I mean to read these Pakistani and American texts contrapuntally, in order, in Edward Said's (1993: 32) words, "to think through and interpret together experiences that are discrepant, each with its particular agenda and pace of development, its own internal formations, its internal coherence and system of external relationships, all of them co-existing and interacting with others." Without asserting any sort of exhaustiveness, definitiveness, or authenticity, these Pakistani texts nonetheless stand in for the excessiveness characteristic of "propaganda by deed" in that they escape the "control" of the worldviews portrayed in and cultural functions served by American spy fiction. Further, I want to emphasize Said's word "discrepant" and the notion of excessiveness I borrow from "propaganda by deed" in order to distinguish these literary analyses, which undoubtedly take as their subject violence and cultural dif-ference, from the stale and staid "clash of civilization" chestnut. Rather than predict or affirm the inevitability of a "clash of civilizations," these analyses, premised as they are on the illiteracy "propaganda by deed" attempts to overcome, look for how the Pakistani texts especially try to "communicate" without exhaustively defining across the chasmal divide so many of the American texts posit between "us" and "them."

My contrapuntal pairing of the post-9/11 Pakistani and American spy novels enacts the argument for shallow reading I laid out in the Introduction. More specifically, my metaphorization of "propaganda by deed" crystallizes the impulses behind shallow reading: this approach focuses on what's expli-citly there in the sense that it concentrates on how the appropriation of spy fiction's conventions by these Pakistani texts alters readerly expectation and encourages a re-evaluation of how these conventions make meaning when deployed in a more standard fashion in the US fictions. The Pakistani texts induce a reflexive "reading" of the spectacular (and popular) representations of espionage, terrorism, and US–Pakistani relations featured in the American narratives. In a manner of speaking, the Pakistani texts' appropriation of spy fiction's conventions encourages a re-evaluation of the pleasures of espionage fiction as a popular or mass market genre. As several critics note, the generic predictability of spy fiction, one of its many readerly charms, offers a prime view of what's visible or has been naturalized, ideologically speaking. Further, the genre's very ordinariness, those elements readers expect and want to encounter between the covers, even when these elements take the form of spy craft and terrorist threats, marks the limits of acceptability. Or, as conventions do in all generic contexts, these elements constrain the content common to spy fictions. Thus, critical attention to these genre conventions and readerly expectations promotes an awareness of what these fictions pass off as necessary and obvious. In the rest of this chapter, I explore the generic limits or constraints that post-9/11 American spy fiction both maintains and alters in order, first, to identify the plain-as-day ideological investments the genre endorses and reinforces, and, then, to suggest why these investments hold appeal. This exploration locates the discrepancies, to echo Said's words, between the American and the Pakistani texts and will, thus, be the sites at which the literary analyses found in later chapters mark the Pakistani texts' intervention. In effect, by locating the discrepancies, I am identifying where and how the American texts are "illiterate" and, in anticipation of the following chapters, pointing toward the ways the Pakistani texts broach these "illiteracies."[8]

With reference to novels such as Rudyard Kipling's *Kim* (1901), Erskine Childers's *The Riddle of the Sands* (1903), and John Buchan's *The Thirty-Nine Steps* (1915), critics trace the beginning of the spy novel to the late nineteenth and early twentieth centuries, locating it primarily within a British context.[9] This time span matters for several reasons. First, this period saw a rise in the production of written materials, in literacy for the emerging middle class, and in leisure time for reading, again for the middle class (Denning 1987: 18; Sauerberg 1984: 4). Additionally, according to Brett F. Woods (2008: 9), spy fiction has "two primary antecedents: (1) the anarchist and terrorist fiction of the late nineteenth century; and (2) Victorian pornography, with its locked rooms, secret amorality, and general suggestion of threat to established values." These precursors show, on the one hand, the role extra-fictional terrorist acts play historically in the genre, thus connecting post-9/11 fictions to the earliest spy novels (and undergirding my interest in reading "propaganda by deed" as a metaphor for the post-9/11 Pakistani fictions). On the other hand, these precursors also help illustrate the changes the post-9/11 fictions bring about, including especially those changes having to do with the blurring of the clandestine and the citizens' realms which helps normalize the state of exception that I explore at length in Chapter 3. Further, this historical emergence, which coincided with Britain's increasing insecurity over the rise of German power in Europe and over its own colonial possessions, marks the genre as one concerned with issues of national power in crisis.[10] American spy novels and films, especially those of the Cold War (the period of American ascendancy in the genre), certainly also bear the strains of national insecurity. Since 11 September 2001, the US as a whole has certainly experienced high levels of national insecurity. Thus, it should come as no surprise that American post-9/11 spy fiction similarly hinges on concerns over national power in crisis.

Yet, ironically, politics occupies a curious place in post-9/11 espionage fiction. Formally, as "ostensibly one of the most 'political' of popular fiction genres" (Denning 1987: 2), espionage narratives deliberately stoke and then mitigate the very anxieties operating extra-fictionally at any given historical moment. Thus, even while these fictions conjure spectacular threats and build suspense, their structural elements, such as narrative pacing, also provide a release of this tension.[11] As Lisa Adams and John Heath point out, "[A]lthough the horrible *ideas* in these books [spy and crime thrillers] might be scary, the *structure* is quite soothing. [... T]he genre's standing promise [is] that the good guys will triumph every time" (Adams and Heath 2007: 65). The narratives' ability to relax the tensions they themselves build marks more a deployment of convention—here, pacing—than any "realistic" outcome to the issues the stories evoke or, certainly, to their extra-fictional inspirations. Locating the genre's ability to satisfy readerly desire in this way matters, because this ability relies on form, not on the extra-fictional politics or history that may inform or simply make recognizable the novels' plots.

With these formal aspects in mind, spy novels help readers navigate through "political" circumstances without engaging with politics at all. Such assurances may be characteristic of the genre throughout its historical existence. Writing about the genre in the twilight of the Cold War, Roger Bromley (1978) identifies this lack of engagement with politics as another of the genre's features. Spy thrillers, for Bromley, are a synthesized romance that draw from both feminine and masculine elements, i.e. from both the purported stasis of the domestic realm as moral safe harbor and the action associated with the public arenas of competition, be it through games, capitalism, or warfare (35). With an explicit Marxist agenda, Bromley goes on to argue that the "lack of a 'consciousness of historicity'" informs the "social function" of the spy thriller as synthesized romance (36). Minus the Marxist impetus to read the genre's "social function" as somehow related to the "real" social conditions that produce it, I borrow Bromley's point to contend that spy fiction's ostensible engagement with "politics" or "history" represents more the narratives' efforts to engage readers than to encourage an analysis of the extra-fictional historical and political circumstances surrounding the stories. As Bromley offers, these efforts, characteristic of much popular fiction, include "the absence of a historicised dimension, with a consequent personalising and individualising of social experience; [... and] the frequent resort to the abstraction 'human nature', and 'universalising' tendency in the presentation of personal relationships" (Bromley 1978: 37). Thus what matters are the values and institutions the fictional spy upholds through his actions, which themselves are abstractions of historical constructions such as "nation" or "democracy." Indeed, David Holloway (2009: 20) classifies the post-9/11 spy thriller specifically as a "molecular instance" of a "normative process" carried out through the "generic welding of stories about state power to the novel's traditional interest in the moral consciousness of protagonists." As Holloway continues, the genre's role in this "normative process" marks it as a "privileged instance in [the] post-9/11 legitimation of torture as a tool for the expansion of human rights" (20–21).[12] At the same time, the personal relationships Bromley mentions take center stage, not any long view of international relations that would aid in the analysis of the conflicts featured in these espionage texts. Consequently, alongside—and often superseding—the values and institutions that motivate the spy are the "personal" drivers of love and family, frequently if not always defined in heterosexual terms, urging the spy through his mission. While "politics," then, does certainly have a role in espionage fiction, it serves as a set piece insofar as the matters of "value," including nation and romance, appear as if outside these "politics."

To return again to Woods's claim that one of spy fiction's antecedents is Victorian pornography, I also want to examine the role of clandestinity as it operates generically on either side of 11 September 2001, especially with respect to how the genre invites readerly identification. Woods's characterization of Victorian pornography—he uses the image of "locked rooms," for instance—instills a notion of separateness: a "secret amorality" and a "threat to established values," both of which suggest an alternative realm from the one citizens inhabit (Woods 2008: 9). John Cawelti and Bruce Rosenberg (1987: 16) reinforce this notion of separateness, asserting that "the clandestine world becomes increasingly shut off from the ordinary world, and its devotees find it more and more difficult to take seriously and even understand the ordinary view of things." The clandestine or shadow sphere that serves as the setting for spies' activities—the intrigue, the violence, the double and triple dealings, the sex—highlights the flimsiness or constructedness of the law-and-order realm in which non-spies live. Indeed, this neat bifurcation of spheres held prominence in pre-9/11 spy fiction when the assumption was that it was harder to tell who the enemy was.[13] Further, as Cawelti and Rosenburg (1987) also claim, this separation, which effectively creates a spectral dimension (hence, "spook") within the citizens' realm, endows the spy with invisibility, a metaphorical state that "frees him of responsibility and gives him license to do things he could not ordinarily do without serious consequences" (13). Early on in the genre's history, this invisibility was one way, according to Lars Ole Sauerberg, that spy fiction engaged readers. The industrialization and urbanization of the early twentieth century helped create a sense of the "masses" as uniform, undifferentiated—precisely what the spy desires to be (Sauerberg 1984: 7). Importantly, though, this uniformity functions merely as the spy's cover, for in this guise, he "is able to turn the scales in international affairs" (7). The result of the spy's ability to be effective even though he seems to be a part of the "masses" is, in Sauerberg's estimation, that "the reader is thus encouraged in his wishes to break away from the world of uniformity" (7). One wonders to what extent this initial encouragement toward identification immured the reading audience to the spy's transgressions. For, as Cawelti and Rosenburg (1987) point out, in the spy's realm, he could act almost entirely without fear of legal or moral repercussions.

The question of readerly identification changes, post-9/11, I contend, to the extent that the clandestine and citizens' realms begin to overlap. That is, post-9/11, fictional and extra-fictional representations of espionage breach this divide between spheres and, thus, change the role of clandestinity in the genre. Readers now "see" the clandestine realm more clearly—if not entirely—than ever before. Knowledge of CIA black sites, drone attacks, Guantanamo Bay detention camp, media scandals and legal proceedings on agents' leaked identities: all these extra-fictional phenomena pervade the citizens' awareness of what would formerly have been the provenance of the spy's shadow world. Given this heightened awareness and in light of my broader interests, a question arises: how do post-9/11 spy fictions represent this blurring of the clandestine and citizens' realms, given both the spy's traditional ability to act outside of standard moral codes and a conventional investment in encouraging readerly identification?

My analyses demonstrate that the Pakistani spy fictions call attention to this blurring, to the dangers of the sanctioned violence following from this merging.

This heightened attention highlights some contrasts. One contrasting way post-9/11 American spy fictions contend with the blurring of the boundary between the clandestine and citizens' realms, for instance, is through neutralizing the ideological stakes of clandestine activities. This neutralization comes about through the genre's "social function," to borrow Bromley's (1978) phrase once again, which continues to depend on readerly identification, even after 9/11. As I have already discussed, a certain irony operates in espionage fiction. With politics as its ostensible raison d'être, this genre appears to be plugged into extra-fictional issues in a more concerted and deliberate way than, say, Harlequin romances. Yet, as critics contend, the "politics" involved in these fictions serve as plot drivers (at the most) and background noise (at the least), given how the very categories of belonging, defined as they are by values, institutions, and the highly vaunted domestic, fictionally exist as though apart from whatever circumstances precipitate the story's action. This apart-ness locates espionage narratives at "a particularly obvious juncture where the codes of ideology and fiction run together" (Woods 2008: 15). Here, "ideology" aligns with what I have been referring to as politics, and Woods's identification of this "obvious juncture" points to the role that popular cultural forms play in ideological (re)production and dissemination. While the obviousness of this juncture abides throughout the genre's history, its persistent presence in post-9/11 American spy fiction helps clarify how these narratives continue to encourage readerly identification as the line between the clandestine and the citizens' realms blurs. Thus, one of the first points about identification to consider is how (successfully) these narratives allow readers to read themselves into the fictions. According to Bromley, this "reading in" process does happen despite the vast differences between the reader's everyday life and the spy's fictional world:

> [A]lthough the content of the experience represented in the fiction is not shared by the reader, the *ideological contexts* in which the reader makes sense of experience are in recognisable relation to the symbols of experience in the fiction: structures of marriage, property, self-image, etc., the status-bearing signs in society.
>
> (Bromley 1978: 34–35)

Scripts that function in a culturally specific manner, such as those shaping how we understand particular societies' "status-bearing signs," render the fictional spy's world familiar enough that readers can stabilize meaning-making and, thus, identify in some measure with the spy.

To postulate such readerly reactions to popular or mass fiction is not to denigrate this reading public. Rather, as Stuart Hall (2010: 76) maintains, such popular cultural forms "are not purely manipulative," as they contain "elements of recognition and identification, something approaching a creation of recognisable experiences and attitudes, to which people are responding." At the "obvious juncture" between ideology and espionage stories, then, spy fictions develop what Anthony Kubiak (2004: 298), commenting on how fictions about terrorism direct readers' meaning-making processes, refers to as the narratives' ability "to construct belief in the [fictional] world." Kubiak's emphasis on the power of mimesis in spy fiction echoes Bromley's points about how readers "read into" such stories. Both critics' points stress how readers' familiarity with the fictional worlds—gained through identification/ the investment of belief—stabilizes meaning-making processes, illustrating how, in Bromley's (1978: 39) words, these fictions exert a "consensualising effect" on their audiences. Thus, while the extra-fictional dissolving of the boundary between the clandestine and citizens' realms heightens general awareness of morally questionable covert activities, fictionally, the emphasis on admirable abstractions apparently distinct from the world of spycraft salves this awareness or, better, the objections to which it may give rise.[14]

Another contrasting way post-9/11 US spy fictions deal with the merging of the clandestine and citizens' realms is through the promise of full knowledge. Insofar as espionage narratives have always relied on threats posed by inscrutable outsiders or double agents, they represent a radical unknowing. In her study of the rise of "fiction of intrigue" in nineteenth-century Britain, Yumna Siddiqi (2008: 1) asserts that these stories "giv[e] voice to concerns about imperial mastery in especially pronounced ways." At the base of these concerns, according to Siddiqi, is the vulnerability of a nation—here, Britain— built upon a colonial system lacking complete understanding of foreign peoples and cultures. The unknowable foreignness so key to these intrigues illustrates Denning's (1987: 13–14) point that espionage novels are "tale[s] of the boundary between nations and cultures." Yet, since, as Allan Hepburn (2005: 11) contends, these narratives both "create and manage crises of belonging," they must also provide a way to apprehend—a word I choose deliberately—this foreignness, to cross or to reinscribe indelibly these boundaries. One way these novels promote this apprehension, according to Hepburn, is via "the repetition of conventions and characters" (35). The familiarity born of repetition, one suspects, assuages the anxiety that unknowable foreignness produces. Indeed, this repetition "engrosses readers" as "formulaic elements" come together in "tightly woven plots" (Bedell 1992: 121). Somewhat counterintuitively, repetition whets readerly appetites rather than slacking them. Further, these narratives' reliance on formula promises readers, Hepburn (2005: 21) explains, the satisfaction of moving out of ignorance into the privileged realm of classified knowledge.

Spy fictions have always enacted this movement toward full(er) knowledge, but, in the post-9/11 American examples, this movement towards knowing involves understanding the foreign in zero-sum terms. That is, the apprehension of the Other in post-9/11 American spy fiction takes on a highly moralistic tone punctuated by the now all too familiar "good versus evil" binary. Several features associated with spy fiction that I have already discussed strengthen the force of this binary: the racial profiling, perpetuated by slogans such as Homeland Security's "If You See Something, Say Something™," which makes the Other literally recognizable but otherwise unknowable or unlike "us"; the absence of history in the genre or its "white noise" inclusion of "politics"; and, relatedly, the readerly identification that occurs via the appeal of abstractions and universalizations, such as shared "values." Together, these features, which themselves blur the line between the extra-fictional and the fictional, diffuse the charge that could result as the clandestine world leaks into the citizens' realm. In other words, the reader faces a choice—informed by the factors I've just listed—between the two poles of the binary, a choice that cuts through any reservations or qualms over the spy's decisions. The reader's and the fictional spy's choices aren't "political" or Islamophobic or biased; instead, they are acceptable "human" reactions in the face of evil. Just as has always been the case, this movement toward full(er) knowledge provides a sense of mastery over the foreign.

My interest in metaphorizing "propaganda by deed" to capture the work I argue the Pakistani novels accomplish via their appropriation of espionage fiction's conventions means to challenge precisely such claims to full(er) knowledge on the grounds that these claims amount to an illiteracy rather than a definitive knowing. A reminder of how terrorism and representations of terrorism are layered interpretations, "propaganda by deed," for my purposes, forces a reckoning with the blurring of the line between the clandestine and the citizens' realms, a genre development particularly evident in our post-9/11 era. Of central concern is how the contrapuntal relationships I build between the post-9/11 Pakistani and US texts help us address the issues that arise as a result of this blurring, especially issues involving the a/immorality of the spy's (and his proxy's) actions. In the next three chapters, I pursue these issues through explorations of the spy, his proxy, and the "terrorist." This trio of figures allows me to lay out a sequence of sorts: the spy, I argue, exerts an affective appeal to the reader through twinned identificatory and revelatory processes; his proxy, who similarly possesses this appeal, represents an explicit expansion of the spy's "sovereignty," which amounts to the permanent incursion of the clandestine realm into the citizens'; and the "terrorist," marked by his appearance, suffers the wrath of the "sovereign," becoming, as a result, a manifestation of the barest of human life. At each turn, I first examine a Pakistani novel to assess its representation of these figures, a move that provides a critical framework intent on identifying the layers of inter-pretation that sediment around espionage fiction's conventions as they're found in my American examples.

Notes

1 My point here fits under Elleke Boehmer's (2009: 149) broader argument about how postcolonial writing can further the study of terror: "postcolonial writing supplies channels for thinking through and beyond terror […], and offers ways of developing workable political responses to its horrors."

2 Walter Laqueur, an important historian of terrorism, is a notable exception here. In Laqueur's view, published in 1998, "propaganda by deed," with its goal of "creat-[ing] as much noise as possible, not to cause the greatest number of fatalities," has faded away. Late twentieth-century terrorism, in Laqueur's view, means "to wreak as much destruction and havoc as possible" (Laqueur 1998: 171–72). My impulse is to speculate over why Laqueur offers such an assessment at that historical moment, i.e. the twilight of the twentieth century. The year of his essay's publication, 1998, saw the signing of the Good Friday agreement between the Northern Irish unionists and the nationalists, which effectively closed the book on the last explicitly Euro-centered/-centric conflict involving terrorist acts as strategy.

3 See also Alex Schmid and Janny de Graaf (1982: 14), who see terrorism as a "combination" of violence and propaganda.

4 See also Arthur Garrison (2004: 260, emphasis in original), who sees terrorists across historical eras recognizing the *"utility of terror"* to convey their messages.

5 Different scholars attribute the term's coinage to different revolutionaries. Ulrich Linse (1982: 201) credits a group of Italian anarchists, including Enrico Malatesta, Carlo Cafiero, and Emilio Corelli with coming up with the phrase. Caroline Cahm (1989: 302) chooses a Frenchman, Paul Brousse, for the honor.

6 See also Schmid and de Graaf (1982: 12) on illiteracy as an obstacle "propaganda by deed" sought to overcome.

7 Sarah Cole (2009: 303) explores a similar point through her examination of the use of melodrama to represent terrorism in literature. For Cole, that genre's "hyperbolic and polarizing structures" demonstrate just the sort of self-consciousness that I argue spy fiction's conventions do.

8 Of course, the Pakistani texts have their "illiteracies," too. One immediate example that spans all four Pakistani novels I discuss is the absence of any mention of religious diversity or minorities in their portrayal of Muslim identity and its connections to Pakistani politics and geography.

9 Brett F. Woods (2008: 1) is the exception to this rule as he identifies James Fenimore Cooper's *The Spy: A Tale of Neutral Ground* as this popular genre's early nineteenth-century American precursor.

10 See David Stafford (1991) for a discussion of this point with respect to the genre as a whole (3) and in British history (7).

11 Jeanne F. Bedell (1992: 116) identifies this build up and cessation of suspense as "perhaps the most widely used ploy in suspense writing."

12 Holloway's (2009) concern with how the post-9/11 spy thriller assists in the legitimation of torture informs my argument in Chapter 3 regarding the representation of the state of exception in post-9/11 American espionage novels. For an analysis similar to Holloway's that focuses on post-9/11 American espionage television shows, see Stacy Takacs's (2012) *Terrorism TV: Popular Entertainment in Post-9/11 America.*

13 The spy's body has always held significance. In a general way, as Hepburn (2005: 12) points out, "The spy's body registers national identities in physical characteristics, voice, and gestures." Such characteristics proved easily mimicked throughout the Cold War both in fiction and in "real life," given "deep cover" agents, for instance. Post-9/11 marks a shift in the significance of the spy's and the enemy's bodies, however, making the bifurcation between spheres less neat. That is, the Department of Homeland Security's "If You See Something, Say Something™" campaign, for example (yes, the slogan is trademarked!), relies entirely on visibility. While part of this visibility refers to "suspicious activity," it also plays out in terms of racial profiling, which means that the enemies' identity isn't as hard to discern, at least in popular post-9/11 representations. This apparent recognizability blurs the line between the clandestine and the citizens' domains. I examine the results of this blurring more in Chapters 3 and 4.

14 See also Allan Hepburn (2005: 35), who argues, "The *frisson* brought on by imperilment reinforces ideology in spy narratives rather than destabilizing belief systems." I take Hepburn's point to be that it's precisely the fictional high-stakes scenarios in which the spy finds himself and in which he must act in immoral ways that cement the bond between the protagonist and the reader. Jeanne Bedell (1992: 121) makes a similar argument about spy fiction's purpose "to elicit certain responses […] through a value system which ordinarily supports the superiority of 'our side'." Both Hepburn's and Bedell's points move beyond identification into the genre's affective appeal, a dynamic that I explore with a concentrated focus on the spy himself in Chapter 2.

2   Spy

A passage from the Gospel according to John, one of the four gospels of the Christian Bible, adorns the face of CIA headquarters in Langley, VA: "And ye shall know the truth and the truth shall make you free." "Truth" and "free," key terms here, putatively justify the fact that spies are master manipulators; they lie for a living. Further, "truth" and "free" resonate throughout the fictions I discuss in this chapter, as these novels traffic in affective appeals and definitive essentialisms. These affective appeals initiate an identificatory process that aligns readers and novelistic points of view, often through the figure of the spy himself (or, occasionally, herself). Simultaneously, this alignment encourages an investment in the spy's or the narrator's ability to define, explain, master situations and, thus, ultimately to reassure through recourse to essentialist tropes; it initiates a revelatory process. Through identification and revelation, these appeals and explanations establish a dispositional starting point that helps make acceptable the zero-sum terms in which post-9/11 American spy fictions cast the Muslim Other, be s/he "terrorist" or not. All told, spies hardly stand as paragons of cross-cultural tolerance or understanding, but they nonetheless manage to cultivate readers' affective attachments to their goals, struggles, and successes.

The appropriation of espionage fiction's conventions, especially those used to represent the American spy, by Nadeem Aslam's 2008 *The Wasted Vigil* draws attention to how the American fictions use these same conventions. As an example of an "excessive" cultural production because it "writes" post-9/11 America from outside, Aslam's novel provides a unique vantage point on the layers of representation at work within espionage thrillers. As I discussed in the previous chapter, the terrorist event itself possesses a metafictional dimension in that, as an act of propaganda, it focuses on audiences and interpretation over and above victims. Terrorism's self-awareness means that representations of terrorist events add layers of interpretation on top of an event already highly overdetermined. Translated to the present task, I contend that the Pakistani fictions bestow a similar self-awareness, induce a self-reflexive reading, as they widen the scope of what 9/11 means. In this chapter, Aslam's novel allows for the critical tracing of the two processes I identify above by highlighting the affective appeals the American spy fictions also issue, as well as the revelatory dynamics they put into play. Here, I explore the interconnected issues involving new developments in spy fiction, post-9/11, and the appropriation of select genre conventions by a Pakistani text, a move that allows us to trace the logic by which the spy's actions become acceptable. In reading Aslam's post-9/11 fiction alongside the American espionage thrillers, I attempt, in Sunera Thobani's (2007: 182, emphasis in original) words, to "engag[e] with definitions of the West *as defined by its others* [so] that the possibility of transcendence of the binary between the West and its Other becomes possible [...]" In other words, this Pakistani novel locates the American texts' illiteracy, wherein the latter rely on an unbreachable divide, a clash in order to achieve resolution. More specifically, through the use of Aslam's fiction as a metaphorical act of "propaganda by deed," the divide I seek to bridge in this chapter pits the putative ahistorical "good" of the spy's goals, both personal and professional, against the similarly acontextualized "evil" or "backwardness" of the terrorist and/or Islam. Both the spy's "good" and the terrorist's "evil" exist plainly on the surface of these texts, as givens that help generate the plots' tensions and suspense, and, thus, my analysis comes about through a process of shallow reading that attempts to account for what and how these surface elements signify when interpreted contrapuntally across the Pakistani and American novels.

In all the novels I discuss here, the identification process depends upon how affective appeals beckon wholeness through freedom. Wholeness derives again and again throughout these novels from romantic attachments, suggesting that romance plots work in concert with the key features of espionage fiction to promote fantasies of national belonging through images of personal romantic satisfaction. This personalization of national belonging hinges upon identification with the spy's romantic desires.[1] Much like how terrorism's metafictional elements, summed up in my previous discussion of "propaganda by deed," draw attention to layers of interpretation and meaning-making, this identification process condenses cultural complexities to achieve what appears a simple end: belonging. Such condensation mirrors Melani McAlister's (2005: 269) understanding of how "[c]ulture packs associations and arguments into dense ecosystems of meaning; it requires us to know a thousand things about politics, social life, and correct feeling in order to 'get it'; and then, in a remarkable sleight of hand, it makes the reactions it evokes seem spontaneous and obvious." In this context, Aslam's novel, for instance, slows the reaction time by isolating and then comparing the identificatory processes that affective appeals initiate. As a result, *The Wasted Vigil* presents the spy's freedom as selfish, controlling, and grown out of convoluted motivations, making the wholeness promised by freedom's achievement appear willfully and dangerously contrived. Read against Aslam's novel, the American fictions' affective appeals frame freedom not just as a defining characteristic of the US—and, thus, a trait under attack by terrorists—but also as a promised wholeness graspable almost exclusively through monogamous heterosexual attachment, which is similarly threatened by terrorist intent. Further, freedom's achievement in these American fictions represents an escape from the excessive threats, violence, and lies of the world that exists as if outside the couple. The couple's security and happiness represent the nation's, a move that masks the historical and political by presenting this security and happiness as universal human "goods."

Truth is the end point of the revelatory process all these novels put into play. Enabled by the identification that takes place via the novels' affective appeals, the revelatory process centers the protagonist's point of view—whether delivered in first or third person—and endows this point of view with power. That is, as I discussed in the previous chapter, spy narratives shepherd the reader through a revelatory process wherein the reader comes to full knowing, even if the spy never does, though this imbalance doesn't infringe upon the identification process. Revelation extends beyond accounting for plot details; revelation works more broadly to exert control, to claim mastery over the geopolitical situation that gives rise to the plot, positing along the way that such mastery is really the guarantee that the good guys will win/have won. Yet, revelation's power over the geopolitical situation doesn't entail an historical reckoning, just as the achievement of the spy's wholeness doesn't either. In the end, revelation relies on fixed essentialisms to provide the security of full knowing, again mirroring how identification passes off the heterosexualized (and, often, US-suburbanized) specific as the universal human norm. In *The Wasted Vigil*, for instance, the spy realizes with a jolt that he doesn't know everything, that someone else holds key elements of the story he thought he controlled. The spy's unpleasant surprise undercuts his authority even as it also demonstrates the cruelty the spy himself exhibits as he keeps elements of the same story from other characters who stake much of their lives on trying to find out these details. Contrapuntally, the American fictions *reveal* truth in earnest, employing an explanatory power, thereby making these fictions capable of dispelling anxiety and re-asserting the US's superiority. These explanations rest upon cultural essentialisms that neatly divide the West from its Other. In its deployment within American espionage fiction, "Muslim," as an essential category, exists alongside (and not necessarily also as) "human" as outside the history that shapes both terms.

The spy's personal brokenness is one of the key features that stretches across these Pakistani and American post-9/11 espionage fictions and that invites the reader to view the spy as more "human." Here's where identification begins. This invitation extends a dynamic Jeanne F. Bedell (1992) observes in much post-World War II spy fiction, wherein "tired men with domestic problems and chronic indigestion [...] have replaced (with the notable exception of James Bond) the indestructible heroes of the past" (120). A boost for "narrative credibility" (120), according to Bedell, the spy's relatability is a central facet, in Allan Hepburn's (2005: 27) view, of "the aesthetic of espionage narrative."[2] Moreover, this relatability contributes to what Roger Bromley (1978: 39) calls popular fiction's "consensualising effect," which is a "mode of inserting the reader, though [the fiction's] various devices, at the level of consent, not just into its 'story' but to its structuring of that story." Bromley's interest in what exists in a narrative beyond the story itself suggests that readers can identify with the spy without actually identifying with the story's plot elements. According to Bromley, the reader acknowledges some "relation to the symbols of experience in the fiction: structures of marriage, property, self-image, etc., the status-bearing signs in society" (34–35). This acknowledgement closes the gap between the spy's fictionally rendered emotional and experiential universe and the reader's, mirroring, not incidentally, the blurring of the clandestine and citizens' realms that has been occurring extra-fictionally in our post-9/11 era. At the same time, this acknowledgement also encourages an investment in structures, such as marriage, family, self-image, that too often appear as existing or occurring outside historical and political contexts, as even immune to historical and political vagaries. The affective weight of the spy narrative, then, lies in the preservation and/or vaunting, as well as the naturalization, of these structures just as much, if not more, than in the vanquishing of the enemy. Or, rather, the vanquishing of the enemy protects the sanctity of these structures, a logic that allows for the enemy to be framed in essentialist terms, as well.

The conventional recurrence of the identificatory process in post-9/11 espionage fiction marks the point at which affect theory can most ably contribute to an analysis of how this genre makes meaning, especially given how this process traffics in essentialisms. Early iterations of affect theory, such as those developed by Eve Sedgwick, who worked from Silvan Tomkins's contributions, and Brian Massumi, who followed through on Gilles Deleuze's work, find unpredictability to be one of affect's biggest appeals. In all threads of affect theory, the body takes center stage. Arguing that constructivist models cannot fully account for the "residue" or "excess" of actual living, affect theorists foreground embodied experience as a critical site of potential change (Hemmings 2005: 549). Moreover, given their interest in conceptualizing the potential for change outside of constructivist models, affect theorists also strive to articulate "an alternative model of subject formation" which gives credence to "*unreasonable* ties" that operate on the "micro level" (Hemmings 2005: 550, emphasis in original). Another common touchstone among affect theorists, according to Clare Hemmings, is "an interest in exploring *analogue* rather than *digital* modes of power and community" or, in other words, the relational rather than the oppositional (Hemmings 2005: 550, emphasis in original). In many ways, this shared interest in the relational emerges as the most distinctive feature of affect theory, for ties between people can be "unexpected," "singular, or indeed [even] quirky," all of which complicate any theory of subject formation that presents itself as "generally applicable" (Hemmings 2005: 550). Sedgwick, in a piece co-authored with Adam Frank, sees this unpredictability as a "productive opacity" (Sedgwick and Frank 1995: 13), and Massumi (1996: 221) calls it "asignifying." Sedgwick and Frank, as well as Massumi, all posit affect as other than psychological "drives" (Sedgwick and Frank 1995: 7) or before emotion, which is an affective response interpreted or made legible (Massumi 1996: 220–21), so to speak, and this distinction is central to their insistence that affect may be able to move critical theory beyond the impasse and determination of social constructivism: affect is unpredictable potential (Sedgwick and Frank 1995: 12; Massumi 1996: 224, 228).

Yet, despite Sedgwick and Frank's (1995: 18), and Massumi's (1996: 223) arguments that their theorizations of affect aren't a return to biologism, other critics contend that their models are too normative, too reliant upon a universalized "human" and, therefore, not sensitive to environment, history, culture, difference, etc. These critics contextualize how affect operates under the weight of history and in specific situations. Hemmings (2005: 565) argues, for instance, that affect may prove critically beneficial precisely because it is "not autonomous" or entirely detached from social constructivism. For her part, Hemmings acknowledges "affect's difference from social structures" but also wants to recognize the "myriad ways that affect manifests itself precisely not as difference, but as a central mechanism of social reproduction in the most glaring ways" (550–51). Hemmings's point about these reproductive tendencies speaks most relevantly to how affect operates in the novels under discussion throughout my analyses. If, as critics of espionage fiction, such as Allan Hepburn (2005: 11), claim, the genre "create[s] and manage[s] crises of belonging" by working out the aliens from the natives, then the reader's identification with the fictional spy, who ultimately helps restore or reassure rightful belonging through the management of crises, amounts to the social reproduction of dominant forms of belonging, which, in the post-9/11 American fictions are presented as "civilizational" or "human" in order to mask their America-centeredness. Thus, the careful examination of the identificatory processes taking place in these fictions—an examination prompted by Aslam's novel's critical portrayal of these processes—focuses on how espionage fiction's common elements, the conventions that readers expect to encounter, reproduce a dominant way of understanding interactions with the Other. It's precisely this understanding that the Pakistani text identifies as a figurative illiteracy, an inability or a failure to engage the Other in other terms.

In Aslam's *The Wasted Vigil*, the American spy's appeal derives from how his professional life takes shape from what Bromley (1978) calls "the symbols of experience" which include family and love narratives, creating a muddle of politics and privacy. Even more, this appeal relies upon the suffering that David Town, the American spy, endures because of his investment in these narratives. David's brokenness reverberates across time and in place, while it also distinguishes his affective appeal in decidedly American terms, a point I develop below, illustrating how the identificatory process reproduces a dominant view of the world. The novel's place-centeredness, as well as its temporal cuts that dial back from post-9/11 Afghanistan to characters' experiences at various locations throughout the preceding decades, isolates the identificatory process that draws readers into this spy's story. The novel's present unfolds in post-9/11 Afghanistan at the house of Marcus Caldwell, an old British man who decades ago married an Afghan woman and lived most of his life in the country. Marcus's house binds all the characters—past and present—together, as his now-deceased daughter Zameen draws David, her former lover, to the site and as the region's history pulls Lara Petrovna, a Russian woman, there in search of information about her dead brother Benedikt, a Soviet soldier killed in Afghanistan in the 1980s. Quite by accident, a fourth character, Casa, joins the trio after he's involved in a compromised Islamist mission to terrorize the adjacent town. Beyond the house itself, secrets spanning the 1980s through to the early 2000s bind these four characters with their simultaneously disparate and overlapping histories, and these secrets drive to the heart of David's vulnerabilities. Neither Marcus nor Lara know, for instance, that Benedikt raped Zameen when she was held captive by the Soviets and that she bore his child, who may or may not be Casa, twenty years before the novel's present. David and the reader know this information, though, thanks in large measure to the narrator's intermittent favoring of David's interiority in the novel's past and present. That is, the novel's revelatory process relies heavily on the authority David enjoys due to his profession, contributing to the creation of his role as an American spy into both a potential locus for the attachment of readerly identification and a site of mastery. David's losses, including especially his loss of Zameen, intertwine with his professional identity and responsibilities, making judgments about his actions difficult to assess as strictly political, say, or justifiably personal. As a result, questions nag at the edges of David's character: do his ideological certainties justify his interpersonal dishonesties? Are these dishonesties generous in the sense that they protect Marcus and Lara from knowing the extra-moral truths to which David alone is privy because he is a spy? Or, is David merely manipulative? Insofar as Aslam's novel asks us to address these questions, it also offers a way to understand how other post-9/11 espionage fictions represent the spy's traditional ability to act outside of standard moral codes and conventions so as to encourage identification.

David's commitment to the CIA, the novel reveals, develops out of an early personal loss. A child of the Cold War, David lived his childhood in an America where "a hatred and fear of Communism was in the air" (Aslam 2008: 112). Even while acknowledging this widely infused anti-communism, the narrator emphasizes that the "disappearance and probable death" of David's brother, Jonathan, in Vietnam, cemented the then fourteen-year-old boy's conviction. Throughout the bulk of the paragraph that lays out David's adolescent history, the narrative voice operates in the third person. The closing sentence, however, slips into first person, as though David himself relays the promise that "for the rest of my life I am going to do everything I can to fuck up the Reds" (Aslam 2008: 112). This momentary shift in voice, subtle and singular, matters, because it breaks down the distance the third-person, omniscient voice maintains throughout the rest of the novel. Functioning like David's direct confession to the reader, this sentence casts what follows, delivered once again in the novel's standard third-person voice, as a possible equivocation:

But that was then. By the time [David] came to Peshawar as an employee of the CIA, his opposition to Communism was the result of study and contemplation. Not something that grew out of a personal wound.

He was in Peshawar as a believer.

(Aslam 2008: 112)

The confessional style of the first-person sentence suddenly renders the knowingness of this third-person conclusion doubtful. Could David's wound be healed by reason and knowledge? The narrator's framing of David as a "believer" during the early stages of his CIA career in Pakistan further clouds the character's motives. A "believer" is not wholly coterminous with one who studied and is contemplative as a result of this considered thinking, but one whose wounds heal through faith might well be a believer, a logic that calls into question the narrator's claim that Jonathan's death does not feed David's anti-communism.

Further, the framing of David's initial anti-communist views as emanating from a "personal wound" illustrates how these post-9/11 spy narratives adapt the conventional identificatory process I discuss above by foregrounding brokenness. Indeed, David's personal history evokes both the dominant conventions associated with American representations of 9/11 and a longer-standing association of victim's discourse with the US's national imaginary. With respect to American representations of 9/11, "ranging from Hollywood film to the pop fiction [sic] and even photography," Muhammad Safeer Awan (2010: 522) calls the invocation of "wound" imagery the "'ideological lynchpin' of the war on terror," wherein the US bases its crusade to defend freedom upon its victim status. David's "personal wound" in *The Wasted Vigil* functions as a metonym for this national wound, putting into play for the reader the dynamics by which the US attracts positive affective attachments to its policies and actions in the "war on terror." At the same time, this personalization supports the idea that these espionage fictions use domestic narratives of family and romance to detach characters from and depoliticize the historical circumstances framed in terms of the wound or an attack on freedom or civilizational principles. Stacy Takacs (2012: 59) emphasizes this domestication by pointing out how American representations of 9/11 presented "Bin Laden's target [not as] the public sphere of US business or political life [...] but the intimate sphere of home and family[, for] his goal was to deprive 'us' of the comforts of (heterosexual) family life." Moreover, the rhetorical deployment of wound imagery or of victim's discourse extends a pre-9/11 trajectory, one carefully traced by Lauren Berlant's work on sentimentality in American cultural history. Berlant (1998) observes that sentiment works to "bind persons to the nation" through identification. In an American context, Berlant contends, "the capacity for suffering and trauma" forms the basis of this collective identification and attachment (636). Significantly, Berlant argues "that this structure has been deployed mainly by the culturally privileged" (636). Through the discursive recourse "suffering and trauma" provide to the privileged in the

US, wound imagery or victim's discourse also signals a figurative illiteracy in how it neglects or refuses to acknowledge the status of the unprivileged. This illiteracy also exists in how victim's discourse insists upon framing history in terms of a vulnerability that must be protected and which subsequently invites and justifies actions—such as regime change, pre-emptive strikes, and enhanced interrogation techniques—that otherwise appear as gross abuses of power. In this exceptionalist realm, affect dominates and collectivizes, ushering in universalist and civilizational rhetorics about "humanness" while actually speaking to only a fortunate group.[3] Thus, beyond the specific questions involving David's earliest wounds and how they influence his later actions, this revelation of David's past also personalizes a broader American discursive dynamic that contributes to an exceptionalist rendering of American history. In other words, the first-person confessional connects readers to David's wound on an emotional level, fleshing out his character's "humanness," even while the narrator insists that such "humanness" is outside the politics that give rise to the histories in which David becomes involved.

David's relationships with the novel's other characters show him to be more than just involved in these histories, however. In fact, as a spy, David helps create these histories, exercising an agency that appears unavailable to the other characters. In the novel's post-9/11 temporal plane, David and Lara become lovers while they are both staying at Marcus's house. Although herself no fan of the Soviet Union, Lara nonetheless repeatedly draws David into conversations about their respective countries' Cold War rivalry, in part to convey how complicated the reasons behind an individual's participation in her/his nation's actions can be. That is, Lara needs to process her brother Benedikt's (unwilling?) role as a Soviet soldier in Afghanistan and, in order to do so, wants to see if David will admit to a complicated relationship with the US's stance during this period. Lara confronts David directly: "'You helped the anti-Soviet guerrillas, the *dukhi*? Yes?'" (Aslam 2008: 80). The third-person narrator indicates that Lara receives no response from David to her question, though the reader knows full well that the answer is "yes." Lara forges on:

> "It's okay," she says. "The two empires hated each other. I know that when Soviet troops entered Afghanistan, the reaction in the United States was, 'We now have the chance to give the Soviets their Vietnam.' Revenge."
> But he is shaking his head. "It's possible that everyone else was fighting the Soviets for the wrong reasons, was mercenary or dishonest, faking enthusiasm due to this or that greed. Even wanting revenge, yes. But I never doubted that my own reasons were good, genuine."
>
> (Aslam 2008: 80–81)

David's response not only individuates his actions but also valorizes them. Whether his "everyone else" refers to the other Americans who assisted the mujahideen, to the Pakistanis, the Saudis, or anyone else, David makes clear that he alone acted on principle. Markedly, however, he doesn't disclose to Lara what his "good, genuine" reasons were. Despite the narrator's tendency to reveal significant details for the reader's private benefit, in this instance, the reader, too, remains uncertain about these reasons, an uncertainty underscored by what the narrator does contribute immediately following this exchange: "Just as it doesn't matter to a person when he is in a hall of mirrors—he himself knows he is the one who is real. The confusion is for the onlookers" (Aslam 2008: 81). The extreme individuation suggested by this image of assured self-knowledge in a maze of reflections mirrors David's own penchant for seeing himself and his motives as unique. Such framing reinforces the broader exceptionalist motif David embodies throughout the novel and heightens his affective appeal as a lone hero who, despite personal sadness, faces adversity bravely. David, to borrow Michael Denning's (1987: 14, emphasis in original) words, becomes "the secret *agent* [who] returns human *agency* to a world which seems less and less the product of human action." In a post-9/11 American context, the symbolic value of this restoration of human agency is high, especially in light of the feelings of powerlessness and vulnerability resulting from the 9/11 attacks.

Further, this restoration of agency helps specify David's affective appeal. In her analysis of the affective power and agency associated with whiteness, Sara Ahmed (2007: 153) asserts that the ability to "[do] things relies not so much on intrinsic capacity, or even upon dispositions or habits, but on the ways in which the world is available as a space for action [...]" In effect, agency is a function available to those who get to inhabit the world *as if* it is a "space for action." In Ahmed's argument, inhabitability depends upon race. Thus: "If the world is made white, then the body-at-home is one that can inhabit whiteness" (Ahmed 2007: 153). Ahmed offers another formulation of the privileges that accrue to select inhabitants via the connections between agency, race, and place when she claims, "[W]hiteness is an orientation that puts certain things within reach" (Ahmed 2007: 154). The "certain things" Ahmed mentions go beyond material objects to include "styles, capacities, aspirations, techniques, habits," as well (Ahmed 2007: 154). In a sense, the world's privileged inhabitants engage in worlding, a continuous (re-)creation of the world so that whiteness remains a "body-at-home" no matter the location.[4] Worlding, then, is mastery in motion. In Aslam's novel, David engages in such worlding when, in the novel's present, he ships from the US the raw materials necessary to build a bark canoe to use on a pond near Marcus's house. In part an exercise in nostalgia, given that, years ago, David dug up the spruce roots he'll use with his now deceased brother (Aslam 2008: 185), and part transplantation of a sanitized and romanticized history, as "David tells Casa [...] that torches would be fastened to the canoes when they were taken out by the Native Americans for night fishing on the lakes of North America" (Aslam 2008: 187), David's canoe manifests the extent to which the world is within David's reach. David's efforts to cordon off his professional activities from his emotions, efforts that are on display throughout his conversation with Lara, to return to my previous example, similarly manifest the world's reachability from David's perspective. At the close of this exchange with Lara, David again stands firm in his conviction that his actions and their motives were just, while also wanting to keep these actions' emotional consequences "a separate matter" (Aslam 2008: 81). David's interest in maintaining a separation between political agency and personal emotions once again posits his wounds as outside history, a location that matters if the idea of "humanness" David's wounds represent is to appear untainted by situational concerns. Yet, the novel's critical presentation of David's agency, which becomes evident through his interactions with others at the house, re-situates his wounds within their distinctly American affective economy.

Put another way, David's reluctance to admit openly to the messiness of his ideological convictions and emotional attachments represents how the novel isolates and then compares the workings of the identificatory process. The wound imagery, the investment in domestic structures and attachments, issue an affective appeal that draws readers into David's character despite the danger of his profession. This hedging over the separation or infiltration of the professional and personal introduces a comparative impulse in that the novel also asks readers to assess the acceptability of David's actions, which reverberate both historically, given his role as a CIA agent in South Asia, and personally in relation to the house's other inhabitants. I've already mentioned that David withholds from Marcus and Lara crucial information about both Zameen and Benedikt. The reader's awareness of David's personal stakes in these overlapping relationships complicates the portrayal of his actions as detached from his emotions. With respect to Lara, for instance, David's evasions and outright lies might just as readily prove selfish as generous. In addition to his unwillingness to concede his compromised position in the conversation I cite above, David lies baldly to Lara, saying he doesn't recall whether Zameen ever mentioned a "Soviet soldier named Benedikt Petrovich" (Aslam 2008: 66). Does David's lie protect Lara? Would it be too much for her to learn about Benedikt's actions while in Afghanistan? Would these personal reasons justify David's dishonesty? Can David be seen as that generous, given that he has the power to solve Lara's mystery, to tell her what happened to Benedikt, but he fails to show her that mercy? Why wouldn't he end her suffering, especially given that his own brother was lost and presumed dead in a foreign land? Do his own anti-communist views prevent him from recognizing someone else's wound? That is, does his American exceptionalism, grounded in victim's discourse, impose or necessitate a myopic vision? These questions drive toward the bigger issue of authority, the authority that justifies David's actions and any readerly affective investment in him. Clearly, David's authority relies upon his control of who knows what, a dynamic that illustrates how the identificatory and revelatory processes overlap.

The Wasted Vigil offers an even more vexing comparison that pulls together identification and revelation as it discloses more details about David's relationship with Zameen. Rather than exploring the ethical stakes of withholding information, this instance focuses on the appeal of saving discourse, a narrative framework that frequently coincides with victim's discourse and similarly possesses strong appeal. Much as with the previous example, David's romantic involvement with Zameen complicates the representations of his actions, since this relationship also pulls together ideological convictions and personal attachments. David meets Zameen in 1980s Peshawar, where he's undercover as a jewel merchant, and she's sought refuge, along with her young son, from Afghanistan. She reveals to him some of the tragedies of her past, including being separated from her parents and losing her young lover, Yusuf, whom she thinks is dead. Upon hearing this last detail, David, the narrator divulges, felt "his heart breaking" (Aslam 2008: 117). As Zameen confides her pain, she tells David she's learned that Yusuf is still alive in a refugee camp, and she enlists David's help in locating this young man, as well as her parents. By the time David locates Marcus, Zameen has died, as has her mother. A chance did exist, however, for David to reunite Zameen with Yusuf. Within a month of Zameen's request, David happened to meet Yusuf at a refugee camp, where the Afghan man offered to translate for the American. For weeks after, David promises himself that he'll tell Zameen about Yusuf, but he consistently fails to do so. While "[h]is conscience ached," David's possessiveness over Zameen and her son, Bihzad, nonetheless prevails (118–19). These plot details reveal that David's initial attraction and attachment to Zameen sooth his persistent loneliness, "the price they [spies] paid for being who they were" (115). Zameen's presence fills the absences in David's life, contributing to a touching romantic narrative that renders David's jealousy understandable.

The acceptability of David's jealousy changes, however, as the novel implicates this romantic narrative in the ideological stakes of the Cold War, the historical event responsible for displacing Zameen and Yusuf, and for motivating David to work for the CIA. When David visits the refugee camp, Yusuf declares his communist convictions, arguing that communism "remains the best hope for a country like Afghanistan" (Aslam 2008: 124). Yusuf's politics convince David that this young man would "only add to [Zameen's] difficulties," a rationalization that feeds David's decision not "to allow this man and his misguidedness to endanger Zameen and the boy" (125). In the midst of these increasingly tangled circumstances, David tells himself that "there was not enough time to get to the refugee camp and warn" Yusuf about an impending Soviet attack there, information about which David gathers through his CIA connections (126). With David's ideological objections already established, the narrator's presentation of David's inability to save Yusuf—an impotency that actually serves the CIA's ends, as they've leaked word of the attack to the international media in the hopes of turning global public opinion against the Soviets (126)—seems less than genuine. Indeed, the narrator's claim proves flimsy as, on the afternoon of the attack, David speeds to the camp upon receiving a note from Zameen in his office in Peshawar that she's just learned that Yusuf is living there. Desperate to keep Zameen from harm, "[o]nly

[David] knows how he managed to get to that camp within the sixty or so minutes that remained before the arrival of the Soviet jets" and, thus, to save Zameen (127). Clearly, David could have warned Yusuf, could have saved him, just as he rushes to save Zameen, which he manages to do.[5] David makes Yusuf a sacrifice to American anti-communism with the same gesture—or lack thereof—that secures, howsoever temporarily, Zameen's emotional dependence and physical affection: on the night of the attack, the narrator reveals, "David became [Zameen's] lover and within days she was half his world" (127). Thus, in the "swept up" language of new love, the novel presents David's role in the attack on the camp as facilitating his romantic triumph, suggesting that the end justifies the means or inviting such a reading given David's relatability. Just as with David's relationship with Lara, a romantic narrative serves as a vehicle to promote identification with a male character whose loneliness seems all the more profound because of his personal losses and the sacrifices he makes to serve the US.

At the same time, however, this romantic narrative implicates David in an old colonial narrative: saving brown women from brown men. By suggesting this dimension of David's relationship with Zameen, *The Wasted Vigil* uses its 1980s temporal plane as a harbinger of the mistakes and violence that will come about in its most contemporary plane, post-9/11. Gayatri Spivak's (1985: 93) articulation of this saving dynamic as it operated in British India highlights the difficulties the subaltern—especially the female subaltern— faces when she tries to utter her "countersentence."[6] In a twenty-first-century "war on terror" context, saving discourse amounts to a cultural chauvinism masquerading as "human rights" or "gender equality." According to David Holloway (2009: 32), the deployment of "human rights" discourses, including those that encompass gender, in our post-9/11 era, often disguises "older loaded terms such as 'progress' or 'civilization,' [as well as] the gamut of racialized ideologies depicting white Anglo-Americanism as the engine of these values [...]" The contemporary usages of "human rights" discourses, especially those that feature the US as defender of these rights, greases the connection between the vulnerabilities characteristic of victim's discourse and the heroism that attends saving discourse. That is, in order for the US to demonstrate its moral superiority, post-9/11, it must use its victim status to fuel its role as righteous defender (avenger?) of freedom, equality, liberty, etc. Through his relationship with Zameen, David becomes the vulnerable savior, a uniquely heroic figure whose appeal seems timeless, placeless. Yet, such a figure develops out of distinctly colonialist and American narratives, which specify David's appeal and point toward the norms and values structuring the fictional universe in which he operates. Insofar as David's appeal ties to these historically and culturally specific narratives, they demonstrate Hemmings's (2005) argument regarding how affect can play a role in the social reproduction of existing structures just as much as it may bear potential for change. The more firmly David occupies a centered position in the novel, the more asser- tively the novel helps make a world David can inhabit comfortably and authoritatively. Yet, *The Wasted Vigil* prevents David's centering, I contend, through its juxtaposed comparisons, which highlight precisely how ideologically motivated even David's most "human" actions are.

Before exploring at greater length how Aslam's novel also uses the revelatory process as a means of consolidating power through the essentialization of culture, I want to highlight the ways in which *The Wasted Vigil*'s presentation of David's wound becomes a critical entry point into how the identificatory process also operates in post-9/11 American espionage fiction. In every American novel included in these analyses, the spy (or, as we'll see in the next chapter, his proxy) suffers from a wound that almost entirely revolves around intimate personal relationships. Paul Patterson, the first-person narrator and spy-hero of Colin MacKinnon's *Morning Spy, Evening Spy* (2006), for instance, suffers the death of his son in a car accident, a tragedy that pre-cipitates his divorce. This doubled loss makes Paul particularly vulnerable and insecure in his new romantic relationship. John Wells, the spy protagonist in Alex Berenson's *The Faithful Spy* (2006), also weathers a divorce and berates himself for being an absent father. Romantic love soured or imperiled also appears in David Ignatius's *Body of Lies* (2007), where Roger Ferris, CIA station chief in Amman, Jordan, tries desperately to extricate himself from a toxic marriage so that he can immerse himself in the true love he's found with an American aid worker who also lives in Jordan. In another of Ignatius's novels, *Blood Money* (2011), much is made of covert agent Sophie Marx's single status—the result, in part, of a messed-up childhood, and presented as a serious problem that finds its resolution by the novel's end.

The recurrence of these wound-based romantic concerns in the post-9/11 American spy fictions marks yet another new development in the genre. In addition to the spy becoming more relatable due to his fallibility, as Bedell (1992: 120) argues, these fictions now also invest much stock in the spy's personal lives. Conventionally, a spy's profession precludes him from having personal attachments, save for sexual encounters usually in service of the spy's clandestine mission.[7] Ordinarily, a spy's existence in the clandestine world, according to John Cawelti and Bruce Rosenberg (1987: 16), bars him from the benefits of a "normal" life, for the clandestine world has "a different lan-guage as well as a different morality." Immersion in this clandestine world results in the spy's inability "to take seriously or even to understand the ordinary view of things" (Cawelti and Rosenberg 1987: 16). In effect, the spy's familiarity with the clandestine world highlights the construction of what passes for "normal" in the "ordinary" world, making civilian life appear naive and/or artificial. Yet, in contrast to Cawelti and Rosenberg's sketch of the paradigmatic spy figure who seems to have no "personal" life separate from his "job" as a spy, many post-9/11 American spy fictions do indeed feature a return to civilian life, thereby suggesting a significant recalibration of the genre's framing of the personal domestic. As these fictions illustrate, the prominence of the romantic love narrative reinstates the spy into a more "authentic" and "human" life—that is, into what's presented as a non-politicized and ahistorical one. The brokenness with which these characters contend and the romantic ideals that they seek align well with a highly conventionalized narrative: the (heterosexual) romantic love story. Such an alignment bears broader significance, as Sara Ahmed contends: "[H]eterosexuality becomes a script that binds the familial with the global; the coupling of man and woman becomes a kind of 'birthing', a giving birth not only to new life, but to ways of living that are already recognisable as forms of civilization" (Ahmed 2004b: 144–45). Romance in these fictions thus serves as a device that links what appears to be personal wholeness to "civilizational good," which amounts to a motivated conception of national ideals projected against a scrim of emotion rather than history or politics. At base, by locating the fictional spy's brokenness in romantic disappointments and yearnings, these American novels enhance the identificatory processes operating within them. Love—or its absence—makes these characters bereft and lonely, on the one hand, and special and chosen, on the other. These fictions thus play out the vulnerability operating on a national scale, post-9/11, in highly individualized, emotional stories, inviting the reader to see the fictional spy's journey toward romantic fulfillment as a metonymic reinstatement of national wholeness. As this formulation implies, the personal nature of the spy's fulfillment also detaches this achievement of wholeness from political and historical contexts, which, in turn, suggests that American national wholeness can occur outside these contexts, as well. Further, just as in Aslam's novel, these identificatory processes show how affective appeals contribute to the social reproduction of existing historically produced and culturally specific structures and values.

Wound imagery or victim's discourse in Ignatius's *Body of Lies* manifests in Roger Ferris's journey from brokenness to wholeness. The body in the novel's title refers to an elaborate plan hatched by Ed Hoffman, Roger Ferris's boss at Langley. Ferris is CIA station chief in Amman, Jordan. Prior to this posting, he's in post-invasion Iraq where he first catches wind of a highly lethal terrorist named Suleiman, "the name of terror" (Ignatius 2007: 28), who's the mastermind behind a series of car bombs across Europe. While outside the Green Zone in Baghdad, Ferris comes under heavy fire and suffers a serious leg injury which leaves him with a limp. In the novel's present, Hoffman's plot, which Ferris aides, is to create the illusion that Suleiman is actually on the CIA's payroll. To do so, Hoffman and Ferris deploy to Pakistan the corpse of a white man and create a legend around it that would force the terrorist leaders in Pakistan who discover the corpse to believe that this man is, first, a CIA agent and, second, Suleiman's handler. Meanwhile, in Amman and other locations, Ferris works to plant the tendrils of this corpse's legend so that their frame job is successful. Amidst all these lies, Ferris meets Alice Melville, an American woman who does humanitarian work in the refugee camps in Jordan. Alice is generous, empathetic, and devoted to doing "good"—three qualities that put her in stark contrast to Ferris's estranged wife, Gretchen, a Justice Department lawyer who is ambitious and self-centered.

In some ways, Ferris is like David from Aslam's *The Wasted Vigil* in that both spies harbor personal injuries that motivate their CIA missions. Jonathan's death cements David's anti-communism, and Ferris's need to redeem the sense of failure that enshrouded his father's career at the CIA (Ignatius 2007: 57), along with his injured leg, feed his certainty that if he doesn't catch Suleiman, it "wasn't the agency's failure, it was his own" (122). By far the strongest link between the two novels, though, is how the spies' romantic attachments salve their wounds and end up re-situating them in relation to the work they do. Of course, the re-situation works to different effects, a contrast the significance of which is made more evident through a contrapuntal reading. Where *The Wasted Vigil* de-centers David's sureties by juxtaposing them against the other characters' questions and complexities, *Body of Lies* reinforces Ferris's self-perception and its accompanying worldview. One of the primary ways Ignatius's novel frames Ferris's romantic wounds is through his deteriorating marriage to Gretchen. The narrative perspective that clearly favors Ferris's view confides Ferris's belief that Gretchen liked the idea of being his wife more than the fact of it: "Being married to an intelligence officer fit her self-image—they were a couple of warriors, in her mind, except that they weren't really a couple" (Ignatius 2007: 73). Ferris finds fault in the idealism bolstering his wife's idea about their marriage: in his view, she merges personal happiness with national identity. Upon learning of his posting to Jordan, for instance, Gretchen "talked about how they were both fighting in the same war, and how they were sacrificing their personal happiness for a greater cause" (64). Ferris rejects this interpretation of their marriage, however, thinking to himself that "nobody stays married because it's the right thing to do for the country" (64). While appearing to provide the counterexample here through Ferris's objection to the merging of the personal, professional, and, ultimately, the patriotic, the novel actually scapegoats Gretchen's perspective in the sense of using it as a foil to make it seem as though Ferris's relationship with Alice represents a completely different—i.e. unpoliticized, ahistoricized—understanding of what love is.

The contrast emerges from the ostensible difference between Gretchen's and Ferris's views of torture. In a scene where Ed Hoffman tells Ferris that the CIA knows more about various terrorist suspects than the Jordanian intelligence agency realizes, Hoffman tips his hat to Gretchen, crediting her work on the "cover-our-ass memo" that places enhanced interrogation techniques in a legal gray zone (Ignatius 2007: 87). By implicating Gretchen in this controversial move, the novel reveals Gretchen's political leanings, which place the perceived safety and well-being of the nation above morally fraught issues, such as enhanced interrogation techniques. Further, the divorce-related plot continues to frame Gretchen as willing to use whatever means necessary to achieve her goal, which, given how the novel portrays her, link directly to politics, while distancing Ferris from such base concerns (Ignatius 2007: 219–23). Ferris does get his hands dirty but only to extricate himself from Gretchen's grasp: in the face of her threats, he digs up personal emails and tax records that prove how Gretchen cheated on student loans and lied about earnings (229–30). While the narrator shows Ferris acknowledging to himself that by countering Gretchen's threat with his own, he's "violated a trust" (232), his dirty work involves revealing Gretchen's perfidy more than his own failings: his is a venial sin compared with her mortal ones. As their ties sever, Ferris remains the one who rises above serious moral and ethical issues, leaving the sense that his marriage to Gretchen wounds him emotionally and morally.

Against this image of polluting or wounding love, *Body of Lies* posits Ferris's new romance with Alice Melville. Nearly every plot detail surrounding Ferris and Alice's relationship underscores a theme of love as escape. The narrator makes this theme explicit via a comparison with Ferris's relationship with Gretchen:

> Not once in his marriage with Gretchen had he wished to hide away with her and let the world disappear. She was of the world; that was the point about Gretchen. She was mint-perfect, coin of the realm. Alice was in another space, still mysterious to Ferris, and he wished he could be there now.
>
> (Ignatius 2007: 120)

The difference in his two romantic relationships frames Alice as something ethereal in contrast to Gretchen's "heavy" value—she's "coin of the realm"— due to her involvement in the world of politics. As Ferris's attachment to Alice deepens, his disaffection with the world Gretchen represents, which includes the lies he must tell for his work, also increases. In order to plan a fake terrorist attack in Europe, for instance, Ferris travels to Rome and calls Alice. "He wished they could meet in Rome, take long walks in the Centro, live on love and the occasional cappuccino, but as it was, he couldn't even tell her he was there" (Ignatius 2007: 165). This relationship becomes Ferris's priority, the narrator reveals, as the spy "didn't care if the new barbarians destroyed every skyscraper in America, so long as they spared Alice" (209). Ferris's willingness to let terrorists strike again as long as Alice is safe makes explicit his re-prioritization: love wins, even over national security. Such a trade-off may seem inappropriate in espionage fiction, but Ferris's preference for his loved one's safety heightens his relatability. Further, the novel allows Ferris and Hoffman to succeed in framing Suleiman anyway, though the success of Ferris and Alice's relationship provides the novel's emotional closure. This doubled success heals both of Ferris's wounds: the one created by his father's failure and the one resulting from his toxic marriage to Gretchen. Ferris's abrogation of his national responsibility remains significant despite these successes, however, in that his need to ensure Alice's safety translates the novel's events into domestic terms. Justice, an understanding of history, a review of foreign policy: none of these points matter as much as the wholeness Ferris achieves through love.

The novel provides emotional satisfaction through Ferris and Alice's marriage. Ferris, no longer in the CIA, joins Alice in her humanitarian work in the region. To ensure their safety, the newlyweds move to "another city in the Arab world, where there was a relief agency that needed volunteers. They didn't tell even their friends where they were going" (Ignatius 2007: 349). The anonymity of their new location signals Ferris's detachment from the political world he inhabited formerly. While the novel closes with the claim that Ferris and Alice "could not escape the enchanting, afflicted culture that had drawn them into its arms, and they did not want to" (349), it does so through the use of freighted orientalized tropes. Indeed, coupled with the anonymity of the city where Ferris and Alice now live, a blankness that generalizes all sites as the same in the "Arab world," this concluding claim naturalizes Arab culture as both "enchanting" and "afflicted," utilizing what Mamdani (2004) calls "Culture Talk" to invest this location with immutable and ahistorical qualities. Yet, the setting matters only insofar as it enhances Ferris's identificatory appeal: his love for Alice requires that he escape from his familiar world, defined by politics, lies, historical events. The vision of national security coinciding with the spy's ability to leave that entire world behind holds out a promise, an appeal that the threats born of political and ideological disagreements can be transcended through heteronormative pair bonding itself secured via conventional marriage. Such an appeal greases the wheels of the identificatory process.

Ferris's happy ending differentiates Ignatius's novel from Aslam's, where Zameen's death prevents David's achievement of wholeness through romantic love. In fact, David doesn't survive through to the novel's end, and while the spy's death isn't entirely unusual—Paul Patterson, the protagonist of Colin MacKinnon's *Morning Spy, Evening Spy*, dies in the 9/11 attack, which takes place at that novel's conclusion—the significance lies in these deaths' legacies. Paul's death in the North Tower of the World Trade Center highlights the intelligence failure that may have contributed to the tragedy (both fictionally and extra-fictionally), but, in doing so, it allows the novel to sound a rallying cry for a reconsideration of how American intelligence agencies operate. In other words, *Morning Spy, Evening Spy* maintains some hope that, with time and work, these agencies may be able to avoid making the same mistakes. While MacKinnon's novel certainly veers much harder into the political realm than does the conclusion of *Body of Lies*, both American post-9/11 spy fictions hold out the promise of wholeness, of recovery from wounds. This holds true for Paul on a personal level, too. In the fourth-to-last sentence of *Morning Spy, Evening Spy*, Paul, acting as first-person narrator, relays that he'll have to return to some of the "fancy stores up the street north of Dupont Circle" after his trip to New York City, in order to "buy something unaffordable for Karen," his new girlfriend (MacKinnon 2006: 304). This mention of Karen so close to the novel's revelation of how Paul dies emphasizes the significance of the romantic relationship at this crucial moment.

In contrast, David's death doesn't offer any promises of wholeness or security. Rather, his death signifies futility: in vain, David tries to convince Casa, the young man who, the novel eventually reveals to the reader, is not actually Zameen's son, to distance himself from the local insurgents. For his part, Casa distrusts all Americans, even David, with whom he's established a personal relationship. In the two characters' final scene, David's grips Casa from behind in a tight embrace, an attempt on the American's part to prevent the younger man's abilities to call out to his fellow insurgents. As Casa struggles to free himself, he "feels along the belt tied to the waist" for a grenade (Aslam 2008: 312). Both David and Casa die in the blast. Unnoticed, Lara witnesses this scene. Having found little closure herself and now newly traumatized by this scene, Lara returns to Russia. Marcus, suddenly alone, continues his search for Bihzad, his lost grandson. The novel closes with an image of the old man's frailty: "He enters the [museum in Kabul] and asks if someone would be kind enough to take him to the city centre in a while. He is meeting someone there who could be Zameen's son" (320). Marcus's continuing search for Bihzad could be read as hopeful in the sense that the old man holds on to the possibility that the younger man may actually still exist. At the same time, however, this image of Marcus tracking down yet another lead could be read as an exercise in Sisyphean absurdity. Such a reading colors the legacy of David's death in a markedly different shade than the legacies following on Paul's. These differences in outcomes in terms of romance and death between *The Wasted Vigil*, on the one hand, and *Body of Lies* and *Morning Spy, Evening Spy*, on the other, point out the disparities between how the identificatory processes are working in these novels. Reading Aslam's novel against Ignatius's and MacKinnon's prompts a comparative analysis that facilitates, first, the identification of the similarities across texts and, second, the speculation over the significance of these differences, especially in the context of how affective appeals can work to reproduce existing values and structures. Aslam's novel features both a lack of resolution in Lara's case and a tragic, nearly absurd repetition in Marcus's. Neither outcome provides the hopeful satisfaction, however laced with sadness, that Ignatius's and MacKinnon's novels do. That difference, made visible through an analysis of how conventions appear in all three texts, points toward the illiteracy Aslam's novel attempts to breach.

As I've shown throughout my discussion of *The Wasted Vigil*, much of the identificatory process that draws readers to a character like David involves David's agency and control over information, which helps him claim mastery over peoples and places. In other words, identification's ability to bond reader to fictional spy depends to some extent on a novel's revelatory process, as well. In espionage fiction, the possession of knowledge is power, and revelation is the journey to full knowledge. The knowledge = power equation historicizes the genre. Taking shape in the late colonial era of the nineteenth and early twentieth centuries, spy fiction, as Yumna Siddiqi (2008: 1) observes, "gives voice to concerns over imperial mastery in especially pronounced ways." The mastery of knowledge and over place then becomes, in Siddiqi's words, an effort "to secure order and intelligibility" (2). Hepburn (2005: 35) also sees mastery as a means of intelligibility, arguing that the genre "promises to conquer otherness." Mastery objectifies the foreign, both place and person, to contain it and, inversely, establishes the spy and the national interests he represents (even when he goes against them in the line of duty) as the norm. Just as identification enacts a worlding, so, too, does revelation, as those individuals who claim to know also claim the ability to explain: their explanations are legible within their familiar structures, institutions, and values. Thus, if the identificatory process trades in faux universals that obscure the debt its narratives of "humanness" owe to American sentimentality, to recall Berlant's (1998) work, for instance, the revelatory process owes a similar debt to essentialism's ostensible ability to explain historically produced phenomena in absolute, unwavering terms. Just as with affect's ability to reproduce existing social conditions, then, the knowledge gleaned through revelation reinforces the familiar or already known. Following the lead of the post-9/11 Pakistani novels, such as Aslam's, I contend that the post-9/11 American spy fictions promote essentialist visions of the Other, again both person and place, as these US texts frame terrorist threats. This recourse to essentialism's explanatory power represents a metaphorical illiteracy, wherein the American spy fictions can't or won't read the Other in any terms other than their own.

Time and again, *The Wasted Vigil* features David deciding to withhold information from Zameen, Marcus, and Lara. As I've already argued, David's decisions to control what the other characters know overlap with the identificatory processes that draw readers to him, intertwining identification and revelation, and blurring the distinction between ideological commitment and personal investment to the point that, despite David's efforts to separate the two, the national interests he represents collapse into his personal desires for wholeness. In the context of an analysis of revelation as an exercise in power, David's objections to Yusuf, for instance, also point toward how the revelatory process relies upon essentialisms that endow the powerful—here, David—with the ability to explain situations authoritatively. Recall that, ostensibly, David determines Yusuf's unsuitability for Zameen based upon the young Afghan's communist convictions, a move that invokes saving discourse along the lines of "saving brown women from brown men." In addition to how this type of saving discourse metamorphoses David from victim to savior, just as the coincidence of these two types of discourse in a post-9/11 American context allows for the triumphant rebounding of a vulnerable and wounded America, the "saving brown women" narrative also reduces "brown" people to naturalized gendered and cultural identities, stripping them of subjectivity and agency in the process. Saving discourse's historical provenance aligns it with other colonial tropes that, according to Thobani (2007: 171), "helped institute and legitimize a hierarchy of humanity among colonizing and colonized populations, and the idea of the superiority of the West was key [...]" One outcome of this hierarchization, Thobani continues, is that whiteness normalizes itself, becoming, in her words, "an invisible 'raceless' identity, [which] thereby equat[es] white subjects and their specific cultural mores and values with the universality of the human" (172). Such "mores and values" include freedom, self-determination, individualism, etc. Within Aslam's novel, these ideas about whiteness converge most explicitly around David, emphasizing once again the structural dominance that allows him to make a world, to act as agent, while the other characters face limitations.

One of the binds of essentialist thinking is that it bars select groups from the possibility of attaining the "mores and values" inherent to whiteness. Placing whiteness at the top of the heap initiates what miriam cooke refers to as the "four-stage logic of empire":

> 1) women have inalienable rights within universal civilization; 2) civilized men recognize and respect these rights; 3) uncivilized men systematically abrogate these rights; and 4) such men [...] thus belong to an alien (Islamic) system.
>
> (miriam cooke 2002: 227)

(Brown) women can traverse the divide separating the civilized from the uncivilized, but only with the assistance of a savior, for, despite having "inalienable rights," these women don't have agency. cooke's formulation of this logic appears to endow brown men with agency; however, once "civilized men" relegate these "uncivilized men" to the "alien system" that is Islam, these brutes are caught in a fixed structure. Mamdani identifies such stasis as a key feature of "Culture Talk." This type of discourse "assumes that every culture has a tangible essence that defines it, and [Culture Talk] then explains politics as a consequence of that essence" (Mamdani 2004: 17). The permanence or immutability of culture's defining structures, such as religion, follow from the assumptions that feed into "Culture Talk." With respect to Islam, "Culture Talk" presumes that Islamic culture was made "only at the beginning [...], as some extraordinary prophetic act," to which Muslims have "conformed" for centuries (18). As a result, Mamdani contends, "history seems to have petrified into a lifeless custom of an antique people who inhabit antique lands" (18). This relegation to the past marks Muslims and places deemed Islamic as pre- or anti-modern (18), a status that can prevent these peoples and places from ever crossing the divide from uncivilized to civilized, but which certainly secures their position within colonialism's and globalization's hierarchies.

Moreover, "Culture Talk" and its variations endow its adherents with the ability to explain fully, to conquer, to claim mastery over encounters with the Other. The essentializing impulses of "Culture Talk," post-9/11, complicate efforts to formulate "political and historical explanations," in Lila Abu-Lughod's (2002) estimation, and, instead, encourage "cultural framing[s that] preven[t] the serious exploration of the roots and nature of human suffering in this part of the world [Afghanistan]" and, arguably, any other location identified by the West as "Islamic" (784). In short, Abu-Lughod advises, "we need to be suspicious when neat cultural icons are plastered over messier historical and political narratives [...]" (785). *The Wasted Vigil* ends by foregrounding such messiness. David's assumption that he knows what's best for Zameen, on the one hand, represents his claim of mastery over her and, given the discursive resonances of this move, over the broader historical and political arena. On the other hand, the disillusionment he experiences when he finds out decades later that Zameen knew that Yusuf didn't die in the Soviet raid on the refugee camp despite his machinations to make it so (Aslam 2008: 284–85) represent the novel's attempt to undermine that mastery. James Pallantine, an American private military contractor and the son of David's CIA mentor, reveals this last truth about Zameen and Yusuf, but the novel doesn't then endow the contractor with any foolproof mastery either. Instead, the narrator makes clear that David allows James to continue to believe inaccurate stories about some of the inhabitants of Usha, the town near Marcus's house (283). In this tit for tat, only the reader has a sense of who knows what, but, because of the possibility that additional, game-changing information may yet be forthcoming, a dynamic made manifest in the exchange between David and James, even the reader is left in uncertainty. That is, revelation in *The Wasted Vigil* doesn't conquer Otherness, as it conventionally does in espionage fiction, where, even if the story doesn't close with the villain vanquished, then, at the least, it identifies with certainty who poses the threat.

"Culture Talk" abounds in post-9/11 American spy fiction, and its premises are rarely if at all questioned. That is, the recurrence across these novels of the essentialism encapsulated in Mamdani's phrase secures knowledge of the Other and, in turn, helps conquer the strangeness, the foreignness, the threat the Other represents. By far the most common trope for "Culture Talk" in these American fictions is Pashtunwali, the code that governs social relations in the tribal areas stretching across the Pakistan–Afghanistan border. This idea plays a central role in Michael Gruber's 2010 *The Good Son*, Dan Fesperman's 2004 *The Warlord's Son*, Ignatius's 2011 *Blood Money*, and Dalton Fury's 2012 *Black Site*. As these novels present Pashtunwali, honor serves as the basis for all social relations among Pashtuns. In *Blood Money*, the third-person narrator explains the motivation of that novel's terrorist as having its roots in one aspect of honor: "Wars begin with *badal*, an assault on a man's honor and self-respect. A proud man must avenge this insult, measure for measure, or he would suffer the greatest shame" (Ignatius 2011: 110). This muscular side of Pashtunwali's idea of honor does not also entail the integrity of a man's word, as the narrator of Fesperman's novel explains through the perspective of one of the novel's Pashtun characters: "upheaval and scheming had long been the norm among [Pashtuns]. You only had to listen to the old songs and poems to know that, verses rife with themes of deceit" (Fesperman 2004: 88). Gruber's novel also conveys its version of Pashtunwali through a Pashtun character, who informs his Punjabi friends, "You cannot, of course, trust a Pashtun, but you can trust a Pashtun to be himself, to do the things demanded by the Pashtun code, to seek revenge, to offer hospitality, and so on" (Gruber 2010: 60). Hospitality serves as another aspect of Pashtun honor, wherein a Pashtun must offer refuge, food, and protection to a stranger while this stranger is in the Pashtun's presence, as the narrator of Fury's *Black Site* explains: "It was an interesting dynamic of Pashtunwali, the local tribal code, that the owner of the property saw to the care of his prisoners" (Fury 2012: 82). A burnt spy in Fury's novel also makes the point that the existence of Pashtunwali means that one can't think of Pakistan's tribal regions as "lawless;" rather, Pashtunwali governs the place via a "*very* strict code" (104).[8] These fictional characterizations of Pashtuns insist upon difference and sameness simultaneously. On the one hand, this code frames Pashtuns as of another type entirely, and on the other, it also homogenizes all Pashtuns across generations, localities, etc. Thus, despite Pashtuns' putatively inherent unreliability, they are knowable, no matter the time, place, or circumstance.

The extra-fictional accuracy of these novels' characterization of Pashtunwali matters little in comparison to how, within the plots, knowledge of how Pashtunwali works equates to power. Gruber's *The Good Son* torques this knowledge to the most extreme effect through Sonia Bailey, an American woman who marries a Pakistani man, travels as a man throughout much of South Asia and on haj, and eventually becomes a mother and then a Jungian psychotherapist.[9] The coincidence of all these roles makes her a prime candidate for CIA recruitment, which happens during the CIA's covert war in 1980s Afghanistan. As an asset under deep cover, Sonia, code name "RING-LEADER," eventually runs an operation called "SHOWBOAT," which entails handling another asset who is also under deep cover as a nuclear scientist who's infiltrated al-Qaeda. The novel's most contemporary plot line involves a conference on therapeutic solutions to the Kashmir crisis that Sonia, as a trained therapist, has convened in her husband's family home in the tribal regions of Pakistan. The conference participants, who include Americans, Europeans, and South Asians, are kidnapped by extremists and al-Qaeda sympathizers on their way to this venue. The hostage situation provides Sonia with the opportunity to assume a leadership position among the captives, as well as to engage their captors. In both of these roles, Sonia relies upon the explanatory power of Pashtunwali and Jungian psychotherapy, and her fluency in these combined essentialisms marks Sonia as the most formidable character in the novel. That is, unlike David in *The Wasted Vigil*, whose use of the essentialist saving discourse gets undercut by his proximity to other characters and by his own personal and political biases, Sonia's reliance on essentializing discourses goes unchallenged, allowing her to appear capable of not only understanding but also conquering Otherness. The revelatory process, as it plays out in *The Good Son*, then, endows the spy—here, Sonia—with tremendous acumen and power, both premised upon a conception of the Other as a fixed entity. The full knowability that revelation promises secures the spy's position as a credible authority.

In order for "Culture Talk" to hold sway, its essentialism must appear an inherent and inescapable quality. *The Good Son* enforces this necessity by making Sonia an expert in Pashtunwali and Jungian psychoanalysis, a field that, in popular parlance, is all about archetypes; in other words, Sonia reads and universalizes cultural practice *as if* Pashtuns were psychologically hardwired to behave in specified and even predictable ways. The novel stresses time and again the psyche's transcendent qualities. In considering her role as a therapist, Sonia sees herself as "reach[ing] deepest into the psyche, below the level of history" (Gruber 2010: 17). Similarly, Sonia must deploy her "colossal discernment" to determine what the "psyche knows, but the psyche is not telling, [for] the psyche is subtle and not entirely of this world" (114). Additionally, Sonia tells her fellow captives that, like Jung, she sees the psyche as "something real going on beyond the scrim of nature" (333). All of these statements regarding what the psyche is, according to Sonia, firmly establish the concept as outside historical vagaries, which, in this last passage, would have a place on the "scrim of nature." Significantly, Sonia also places *certain* cultures, including Pashtun culture, outside such vagaries, too. In response to another hostage's question about how Sonia is interpreting the dreams of her captors, for instance, Sonia claims that, since "traditional Muslims" are like American Indians and Chicanos in that they are all from "highly traditional cultures," they can all be treated, psychologically speaking, in similar ways. Thus, according to Sonia's reasoning, the dreams of members of these populations possess common elements, which only she, as a trained therapist, can understand. Notably, Sonia groups together populations that are in uneven power relationships with the US, and she asserts her mastery over their cultures, each different but, in effect, the same in their difference. Further, Sonia jumps from speaking strictly of Pashtunwali to encompassing all "traditional Muslims," lumping together yet more diversity under a single heading. As a site of authority, Sonia contains each of these other cultures within a homogenizing label, which facilitates her knowledge and, hence, exercise of power over them.

Indeed, Sonia's mastery is so complete, her fluency in both Pashtunwali and Jungian psychotherapy so advanced, that she can exert control over her dangerous captors. Her plan is to interpret their dreams so as to enact a sort of reverse Stockholm Syndrome—i.e. to get the captors to sympathize with the captives (Gruber 2010: 94). One of Sonia's first "patients" is a Pashtun guard named Patang. In her interpretation of Patang's dream, Sonia predicts that he'll hurt his foot. When one of her fellow captives questions how she could know the future, Sonia replies, "Because he dreamed it and I interpreted the dream that way" (119). Thus, as Sonia goes on to explain:

> "Patang will be thinking about his foot all the time now. He'll be extra careful for a while, but it will gnaw at him, he'll grow clumsy [...] Or he'll become so obsessed with the idea that he'll unconsciously discharge the tension by 'accidentally' dropping a load of bricks on his toes. Then,

naturally, he'll blab the whole thing. Pashtuns are fascinated by this kind of stuff; it's threaded through all their folktales—the prophetic dream."

(Gruber 2010: 120)

With its use of adverbs—"unconsciously," "accidentally" in scare quotes, and "naturally"—this passage outlines the power Sonia derives from her essentialist assumptions about the other. Her psychological expertise makes her certain of how Patang will process her interpretation of his dream, as if there is only a single way this process will play out. Moreover, Sonia knows Patang is doubly susceptible to her power, because he's Pashtun, and they can't help but be pulled into such beliefs. By ascribing such credulity to Pashtun culture, Sonia's explanation exemplifies one of Mamdani's (2004) points about how "Culture Talk" works: Muslims can only conform to culture, not make or change it. In this way, Patang and the other Pashtuns can't think for themselves, much less exercise agency outside of their culture's prescriptions. Needless to say, Patang does hurt his foot, validating Sonia's interpretation and encouraging everyone, including the other captives, to believe that Sonia does indeed hold power, because she knows everything.

Sonia's interpretation of dreams grants her control over the Other. At the same time, the knowledge and power she exercises efface historical considerations. Just as with Patang, every dream Sonia interprets comes "true." When the leader of the captors, a man named Idris, comes to have his dream interpreted, Sonia rebuffs his questions about how she could know what his dreams mean by saying, "'You would not understand if I told you'" (Gruber 2010: 239). The narrator, favoring Sonia's interior, then adds, "It was a reasonable guess, she thinks, with some satisfaction. Men in patriarchal cultures who are under extreme psychological stress often have anima dreams, as the suppressed female principle in them struggles to break out" (239). Again, Sonia's approach conflates (suspect) psychology and culture to create an explanation with an air of the inexorable. Although Sonia acknowledges that Idris is under stress, she doesn't explore that force's dynamics, an exploration that would necessitate a consideration of specific and variable contexts and pressures—that is, a consideration of politics and power. Sonia demonstrates a similar disregard for how historical concepts—rather than totalizing ideas of culture—can shape action and meaning when she shares with the other captives her views on Islam:

"Islam is a very decentralized religion. Anyone can call himself a mujahid, a holy warrior. The movement attracts lots of people, from the sincerely religious to the insane or just bored kids looking for action. In the West they race cars or knock off convenience stores. Here they become mujahideen."

(Gruber 2010: 91)

The lines of causation Sonia draws here stretch credulity. Her explanations for what motivates Muslims to become mujahideen run the gamut from "all devout

Muslims are extremists" to "if only these boys had a hobby… " History, speci-ficity, politics, power: all are noticeably absent from Sonia's account. The tendency of Sonia's explanations to efface politics and power demonstrates how "Culture Talk" relies on immutable essences that seem to exist outside time and place. Duly contained, the Pashtuns and the Muslims of Gruber's novel don't possess the dynamism, the unpredictability, the potential that living "in" history entails.

Sonia's explanations consistently reveal some crucial aspect of Pashtunwali or Islam in general. Her fellow captives and even her captors come to see Sonia as powerful and in control. The curious mix of psychotherapy and cultural essentialism that converge in *The Good Son*'s version of "Culture Talk" produces an idea of identity as recognizable as the "humanness" the identificatory process also constructs. However, whereas identification's "humanness" purports to be universal when it's actually specific, the identity that emerges through the deployment of "Culture Talk" represents an unchanging difference that exists outside the universal. The identificatory process, which makes visible the spy's appeal and consolidates the reader's investment in what the spy represents, and the revelatory process, which relies on a knowledge = power equation that situates the spy as a site of authority and which also contains or controls the Other, function in a complementary manner that renders the spy's actions acceptable.

These analyses foreground the twinned processes of identification and revelation that I argue are central to cultivating readerly investment in the figure of the spy, as well as in the spy's perspectives and actions. Aslam's *The Wasted Vigil* exemplifies the contrived and even dangerous facets of the identificatory process—or what Sara Ahmed (2004a: 130) calls "fellow feeling"—through its presentation of David's anti-communism, for instance, alongside Lara's struggles to understand her own and her brother's positions in the Soviet Union. Further, *The Wasted Vigil* also shows David's inability to con-quer Otherness not just through his failed attempts to "save" Zameen but also through his inability to control and to know entirely the circumstances of her life. That the American fictions lack such a critically comparative impulse but possess a knack for conquering Otherness becomes evident when read against Aslam's novel; in other words, Aslam's novel locates the American fictions' illiteracies. With the insights gleaned from this Pakistani novel, we see more readily how Ignatius's and MacKinnon's novels, for example, feature only the emotional transmogrification from victim to savior, from wounded to wholeness, accomplished through romantic love. Similarly, David's fallibility, unknown to him but evident to readers, encourages a questioning of Gruber's representa-tion of Sonia, especially in her reliance on essentializing discourses that allow her to claim mastery over the Other. The recurrence of these processes across both the Pakistani and American post-9/11 spy fictions matters because, as I argue in the next chapter, it expands to encompass the spy's proxies—the private military contractor and the Special Forces Operator—and, to normalize the blurring of the clandestine and citizens' realms, a dynamic that extends the spy's covert powers to citizens and military personnel who are supposed to be held to established and explicit moral codes and laws.

Notes

1 Similarly, Gargi Bhattacharyya (2008: 8) argues: "In the face of terrorist attacks that despise 'our way of life,' our way of life comes to be represented as a familial drama, all idealised gender types and affective relations." She goes in another direction, however, wondering if such idealizations are meant to suggest that "'we' feel and they do not."

2 Hepburn's (2005) view of espionage fiction's identificatory process differs from Bedell's and my own. For Hepburn, who concentrates on twentieth-century representations (and, thus, pre-9/11 ones), the spy's "authenticity may be irrelevant [as the] spy's identity is often an illusion" (xiv). In the post-9/11 American spy thrillers I discuss here, the narratives' entire thrust relies upon the spy's authenticity, if not wholly with respect to US politics or foreign policy than with respect to his "personal" identity. Indeed, many of these fictional spies want nothing more than to find a refuge where they can be their authentic selves, a desire that, I argue, resonates with readers of this popular genre.

3 My use of the term "exceptionalist" here connects my point to that critical mainstay in American Studies. In Chapter 3, I focus on another type of "exception," which puts American exceptionalism in stark relief.

4 I mean to invoke Gayatri Spivak's (1985: 235) use of the term "worlding" from "Three Women's Texts and a Critique of Imperialism," even as she "vulgarizes" Heidegger's usage (235). Also, see Ahmed (2007: 154) for a discussion of how "whiteness" is inherited.

5 David later learns that Yusuf somehow manages to survive the attack, an outcome which, from both the reader's and the character's perspectives, puts a chink in the armor of David's omniscience and agency (Aslam 2008: 284–85).

6 If this subaltern isn't drowned out by the dominant and opposing factions claiming to speak for her, she's stymied to find a discursive model that doesn't already predetermine her utterances. Malini Johar Schueller (2009: 243) also identifies the colonial trope of framing colonized peoples as "children in need of rescue" as another instance of saving discourse. As Schueller points out, in this instance, too, saving discourse contributes to "the construction of the western polis" and, thus, Western notions of subjectivity and superiority.

7 I use the masculine pronoun, because the majority of the novels I discuss feature male spies. Only Sophie Marx from Ignatius's *Blood Money* is the exception as a female in this discussion of romantic love. However, she, too, travels the distance of the romantic love narrative in a highly gendered and prescribed way.

8 In Chapter 3, I explore the expansion of this cultural essentialism into the realm of politics and the nation, an expansion that allows these novels' representation of Pakistan and Pakistanis to be read culturally rather than historically or politically. The conflation between culture and nation, made possible by essentialist readings, facilitates the conversion of the place of the nation into a state of exception, a zone wherein Pakistani national sovereignty holds no meaning.

9 Sonia's only remaining child is her son, Theo, who becomes a celebrated mujahideen during his adolescence and, later, a Special Forces Operator in the US military. Gruber's novel thus inhabits a unique position among the post-9/11 novels I discuss in that it balances both the spy and, in this instance, her proxy.

3   Proxy

Recently, I found myself in conversation with a Major in the US Army who had just returned from his second tour in Afghanistan. The Major, who works in military intelligence, told me that his job in Afghanistan was to forecast a plan for the next ten years. From a military perspective, he said, the priority is to ensure that Afghanistan has a strong enough military to stabilize its government. The Major listed what tasks fall under this priority—they include proper tactical and procedural training, for example—and ended with the goal of inculcating within the Afghan military establishment the understanding that they need to root out al-Qaeda and other terrorist organizations should they ever try to set up operations within Afghanistan again. I could see, I said to the Major, how just about any country would want to achieve the stability the US Army was valuing here, but, I said, I wondered about that last item. What if an Afghan government sees "terrorist organizations" differently from the US?

In that case, the Major told me, the US military would have to go in and "mow the grass. Just like we did in Pakistan."

The Major's reference to Pakistan obviously concerns the 2011 Navy SEALs raid on Osama bin Laden's Abbottabad compound. His metaphor, though, makes both the Pakistan reference and the Afghanistan context particularly striking. Drive through any American suburb on a Saturday during the months of April to September, and countless people will be mowing the grass. Doing so is an exercise in domestication, in tidying up the small or large plot of land upon which one's house sits so that the yard looks orderly. Some more exclusive communities actually stipulate how frequently one's lawn must be mowed, for, in these communities, too-tall grass is unsightly. Often in such communities, crews of immigrants—legal and not—carry out this task for the privileged homeowners. As a metaphor, to "mow the grass" suggests that the US views Pakistan and Afghanistan as its yard, that these yards may get overgrown, and that the US has a responsibility to keep both yards tidy, through their own work or via labor contracted for the job. This metaphorical expansiveness further suggests that the US can disregard Pakistan's and Afghanistan's sovereignty or, to put it another way, can breach these nations' sovereignty to accomplish what the US deems a larger "good," irrespective of Pakistan's or Afghanistan's viewpoints. Just because the metaphor invites it, the American suburban sheen associated with the activity of mowing further asks us to consider who benefits from this American appropriation of the mowing responsibilities; that is, what type of norm does "mowing" reinscribe? Any attempt to address this question needs to take into account who mows, as well as his relation to the places directly and indirectly involved and to these places' inhabitants.

My reading of the Major's metaphor introduces this chapter's focus on questions of sovereignty, including especially who acts as sovereign and what their relation to places and peoples subject to the sovereign's power is like. This focus helps me develop further two of the interconnected issues I mention in the Introduction: first, how the emergence of the spy's proxy marks a change in spy fiction as a genre; and second, how the Pakistani appropriation of generic conventions highlights the logic through which the conditions brought about via the sovereign's power become acceptable. Here, I examine the rising prominence of the private military contractor (PMC) and the Special Forces Operator in post-9/11 espionage fiction. These two figures serve as the spy's proxy, often acting on intelligence provided by the CIA or doing an end run around the usual intelligence channels to take on roles previously occupied solely by CIA agents. Both Aslam's *The Wasted Vigil* (2008) and Kamila Shamsie's *Burnt Shadows* (2009) feature PMCs that have strong ties to the CIA. Additionally, Gruber's *The Good Son* (2010) has a Special Ops soldier working alongside a CIA asset, but other novels, including Dalton Fury's *Black Site* (2012), Colin MacKinnon's *The Contractor* (2009), and Ben Coes's *Coup d'État* (2011), center the contractor or Special Forces Operator, eclipsing entirely the expected spy while still endowing these proxies with many of the spy's conventional characteristics. These proxy fictions put into play the significant paradigm shift the US's "war on terror" has enacted. As Pulitzer Prize-winning journalist Mark Mazzetti asserts in *The Way of the Knife*:

> Prior to the attacks of September 11, the Pentagon did very little human spying, and the CIA was not officially permitted to kill. In the years since, each has done a great deal of both, and a military-intelligence complex has emerged to carry out the new American way of war.
>
> (Mazzetti 2013c: 4–5)

The "military-intelligence complex," as Mazzetti phrases it, encapsulates the blurring of the line between the clandestine and citizens' realms that I've been discussing. This blurring provides a negative answer to a question posed by Giorgio Agamben (1995: 5–6), as he considers the visibility of what he refers to as the sovereign's power: "Confronted with phenomena such as the power of the society of the spectacle that is everywhere transforming the political realm today, is it legitimate or even possible to hold subjective technologies and political techniques apart?" This question, which the balance of Agamben's volume also answers in the negative, draws attention to the visible with its reference to the "society of the spectacle," reaffirming the need for shallow reading. Indeed, Agamben's observation of "the power of the society of the spectacle" resonates with the concept of "propaganda by deed." My meta-phorization of this concept, carried out via the contrapuntal reading of post-9/11 Pakistani and American spy fictions, works in this chapter to highlight the singularity of the proxy's position in the genre and, as significantly, in the larger discursive fields to which cultural productions such as spy fictions contribute. The emergence of the spy's proxy, including drones, stands as the high-water mark of what can be seen as the clandestine and citizens' realms converge. Both fictionally and extra-fictionally, readers "see" the positions the spy's proxies occupy, and Shamsie's *Burnt Shadows*, the Pakistani text on which I focus most intently in this chapter, re-frames the American fictions' largely heroic portrayals of the proxy as a type of illiteracy that fails to read the implications of this visibility.

My discussion of the spy in the last chapter introduces how that figure comes to act as sovereign: not just through the demands of a given mission but also through his ability to draw the reader to his perspective and values. In this chapter, I emphasize how the ability to act as sovereign expands to non-covert actors, an expansion that emblematizes the normalization of the sovereign's use of power, which becomes visible through the blurring of the clandestine and citizens' realms. This visibility comes into focus through the spy's and the proxy's relation to place and its peoples. According to Mazzetti, as the contractor and the Special Forces Operator come to act as spies—and spies as soldiers—the more their reach and activities (if not the specifics of their reach and activities) gain public visibility. The post-9/11 spy fictions I discuss here engage the same dynamic. The merging of the clandestine and citizens' realms accomplished by the creation of the "military-intelligence complex" and the ways this merging makes their activities more visible brings to the fore questions of the acceptability of the actions represented in these texts, especially those that appear to legitimate the use of state violence against the Other.

As I argued in the previous chapter, the identificatory and revelatory processes that combine to construct the spy's affective appeal position this figure as relatable and authoritative. The spy's proxies embody many of the same characteristics, including bearing wounds and mastering place and the Other. Harry Burton from Kamila Shamsie's *Burnt Shadows* suffers from lost origins, having been removed from "his" India just as the sun was setting on the British Empire, as well as from a distanced relationship with his daughter, Kim. My analysis of Harry that follows demonstrates how the proxy's particular appeal links to sovereign power and the transformation of place into a state of exception. Harry's example recasts the post-9/11 American fictions that share these same conventions. In Coes's *Coup d'État*, for instance, Dewey Andreas, the former Delta who is the only one who can spearhead the US government's regime change in post-9/11 Pakistan, is haunted by lost comrades and hunted by "terrorists" seeking revenge. Theo Laghari, Special Operations soldier in Gruber's *The Good Son*, is literally wounded on a mission in Afghanistan; plus, he has mommy issues, even though his unique upbringing provided him with the skill set necessary to succeed in the novel's highly dangerous mission. Rick Behringer from MacKinnon's *The Contractor* can't quite cope with his divorce, nor with the suicide of his father, a former CIA agent, but he infiltrates foreign and terrorist intelligence networks like no one in the CIA can. Finally, Kolt Raynor, the Delta protagonist of Dalton Fury's *Black Site*, nearly drinks himself into oblivion after his poor judgment call results in the deaths of his men, but, with some training and restored faith in himself, he manages to save several other Deltas held captive by tribal unfriendlies. At the conclusion of all these American fictions, the contractor or the Special Forces Operator re-centers himself personally: Dewey consummates his romantic relationship with Jessica Tanzer, the US National Security Advisor; Theo learns the truth about his mother's involvement in the CIA; Rick reconciles with his ex-wife; and Kolt saves his best friend, feared dead, from Taliban-al Qaeda captivity. Like the conventional spy in espionage fiction, these proxies also draw the reader into the narratives via identification, and their elite or exceptional skills facilitate their mastery or control even as they function as a revelation of a different sort; in addition to benefiting from both human and communications intelligence, they can take care of business, because they are highly trained individuals.

In possession of the same appeal as the spy, the proxies featured in these post-9/11 fictions also contribute to the merging of the clandestine and the citizens' realms by virtue of the fact that they are not CIA and, theoretically at least, inhabit the same sphere with the same norms and values as the citizen. At the same time, the proxy's actions blur the distinction between violence and law, making it "impossible to distinguish transgression of the law from execution of the law, such that what violates a rule and what conforms to it coincide without any remainder" (Agamben 1995: 57). In this way, the proxy, who acts like the spy, also acts as sovereign, the very figure who can transgress the law as he executes it. The sovereign's actions, as Agamben continues, are undertaken to "safeguar[d] the existence of [a specific] norm and its applicability in [a specific] normal situation" (31)—i.e. the citizens' realm that excludes those abandoned by the sovereign's law or, put another way, relegates the abandoned to a state of "bare life," an intense vulnerability wherein the individual is at the same time subject to the law but denied its protection. Through their safeguarding functions, furthermore, the sovereign's actions gain acceptability in this "normal" and exclusive situation. The sovereign suspends law to protect the order that law creates, implicating those who benefit from that order, i.e. when the sovereign's exercise of power is done for their collective "good." Moreover, sovereignty also operates implicitly in relation to place. Thus, this expansion of sovereignty to encompass the contractor (a civilian purported to be bound by all laws applicable to citizens) and the Special Forces Operator (a serviceman ostensibly bound by military code) allows these two figures to act with moral and legal impunity, just as the spy does. Insofar as the spy and his proxies exert affective appeal and demonstrate control and power through knowledge, their im/amoral actions gain acceptance as "necessary" and, perhaps, even "good." Identification and revelation reaffirm the sovereign's power and, implicitly, his relationship to place—both the place where law is suspended and the place where the law appears to be in force— normalizing the violence resulting from the sovereign's exertion of power. The very fact of the proxy's involvement in the exercise of sovereign power, often as the sovereign himself, increases the visibility of how this type of power operates. That is, the proxy as a figure signals the blurring of the clandestine and citizens' realms, making the expansion of the sovereign's reach plainer to see.

This phenomenon, wherein the norms and values operating in the clandestine realm grow more acceptable as they seep into the citizens' realm, speaks to my interest in expanding the discussion of affect I initiated in the previous chapter. For all affect's theoretical potentiality, made possible by the phenomenon's embodiedness, Clare Hemmings (2005: 550–51) cautions that our interpretation or understanding of affective responses may nonetheless assist in the work of social reproduction or the maintenance of the status quo. Although not in direct or explicit response to affect theorists such as Tomkins, Deleuze, Sedgwick, or Massumi, Agamben does devote considerable energy to the body as a potential site of change. In *Homo Sacer*, for instance, Agamben announces the need to be more "cautious" when theorizing the body, for it is:

> always already caught in a deployment of power. The "body" is always already a biopolitical body and a bare life, and nothing in it or the economy of its pleasure seems to allow us to find solid ground on which to oppose the demands of sovereign power.
>
> (Agamben 1995: 187)[1]

Both the concept of the biopolitical body, derived from Michel Foucault's notions of the disciplined body, and the concept of "bare life," upon which Agamben bestows much attention, serve as key features of Agamben's theorization of the body's enmeshment in power. In *Homo Sacer* and in *State of Exception*, Agamben examines the threshold "between the juridico-institutional and the biopolitical models of power," insisting that the "two analyses cannot be separated" (Agamben 1995: 7). The "biopolitical body" obviously fits in the "biopolitical" model of power, a model that relies on Foucault's definition of self-discipline. "Bare life," rather than aligning exclusively with juridico-institutional models—the concept of the rights-bearing citizen is more apt here—functions as the concept Agamben employs for the body, the person, who only appears as if he exists outside of a given order and whom Agamben identifies as *homo sacer*. While not completely nihilistic, Agamben's insistence on the foundational presence of "bare life" significantly qualifies how the body's affective potential or "naturalness" can work to undermine existing structures.[2] Instead, Agamben's "bare life" inducts considerations of the body into the sovereign's realm wherein both the juridico-institutional and the bio-political operate, creating the possibility of what Agamben terms the "state of exception."

The state of exception, along with sovereignty and "bare life," schematize, first, the ideas of affective appeal issued through identification and, second, the trust in the spy and his proxies secured through the revelation of knowledge, which itself is a way to contain or conquer the Other. The state of exception and Agamben's formulation of sovereignty rely on "bare life." Most basically, according to Agamben (1995: 15), the sovereign is "at the same time, outside and inside the juridical order." Yet, neither politics nor the "juridical order" contains the sovereign and his power. Instead, Agamben (1995: 28) argues, sovereignty is "the originary structure in which law refers to life and includes it in itself by suspending it." The sovereign validates the law by suspending it or through applying it differentially so that the law establishes order for some and "abandons" others to "bare life." The legitimacy of this order takes shape through the Others' differential relation to the law—their abandonment by the law—a relation determined, as I've indicated, by the sovereign. This twinned idea of inclusivity and exclusivity creates the "sovereign exception" or the state of exception, and "bare life" characterizes the status of those excluded within the exception. In Agamben's framework:

> The exception is a form of exclusion. [... T]he most proper characteristic of the exception is that what is excluded in it is not, on account of being excluded, absolutely without relation to the rule [of law]. On the contrary, what is excluded in the exception maintains itself in relation to the rule in the form of the rule's suspension. *The rule applies to the exception in no longer applying, in withdrawing from it.*
>
> (Agamben 1995: 17–18, emphasis in original)

As I've hinted, Agamben (1995: 28–29, 181) later calls this withdrawal an abandonment, and the sovereign's ability to abandon those who are excluded from the law, those reduced to "bare life," constitutes his greatest power.

The banned person, Agamben's (1995: 28–29) *homo sacer* who lives "bare life," exists in this curious relation to the law and is, thus, "exposed and threatened on the threshold in which life and law, outside and inside, become indistinguishable."[3] Given his interest in locating this threshold or "zone of indistinction (or at least the point of intersection)" (5–6), Agamben adds a place-oriented dimension to his theorization of sovereignty so as to specify (if not entirely historicize) where juridico-institutional and biopolitical power converge.[4] Thus, the banned person lives in a state of exception, a "complex topological figure in which not only the exception and the rule but also the state of nature and law, outside and inside, pass through one another" (Agamben 1995: 37).[5] Moreover, the banned person's vulnerability results from the sovereign being "the point of indistinction between violence and law, the threshold on which violence passes over into law and law passes over into violence" (Agamben 1995: 32). The indistinction between violence and law creates the conditions that allow the "legitimate" use of violence against those excluded from the law and, relatedly, the benefits that accrue to those included, for, as Agamben claims, the law "nourishes itself on this exception and is a dead letter without it" (Agamben 1995: 27). The sovereign's power reinforces a well-nourished law, creating along the way an atmosphere of acceptability of the resulting norms.

Within post-9/11 espionage fictions, these norms and their acceptability come about through the expansion of sovereignty. Further, these novels call forth extra-fictional phenomena in their representation of this expansion. Having marked this new paradigm with his phrase "military-intelligence complex," Mazzetti (2013c: 6) goes on to claim that it "turned the American president into the final arbiter of whether specific people in far-off lands live or die." In other words, the American President now exercises a sovereignty, in Agamben's use of the word, over "bare life" in an explicit manner. In Agamben's own work, he traces the expansion of sovereignty to physicians and scientists, an expansion he recognizes as worrisome while nonetheless characteristic of our present era (Agamben 1995: 159). This chapter's fictional examples continue this expansion, endowing the spy's proxies with the sovereign's power. Such expansion hastens the blurring of the clandestine and citizens' realms or fictionally animates Agamben's observation:

> What happened and is still happening, before our eyes is that the [...] state of exception [...] has transgressed its spatiotemporal boundaries and now, overflowing outside them, is starting to coincide with the normal order, in which everything again becomes possible.
>
> (Agamben 1995: 38)[6]

This coincidence amounts to the seepage of the clandestine into the citizens' realm to which I've been referring. The acceptability of what Agamben refers to as a "transgression" comes about through a cumulative process facilitated by both the spy's and the proxy's appeal.

Both Nadeem Aslam's *The Wasted Vigil* and Kamila Shamsie's *Burnt Shadows* include military contractors who act as the spy's proxy. The Pakistani appropriations of this increasingly stock character in post-9/11 American espionage fiction point toward an illiteracy at the base of the sovereign's agency. Much like the worlding apparent in David's interactions with the other characters and with place in Aslam's novel, the sovereign acts meaningfully and at the expense or in the absence of others' abilities to do the same. Through Harry Burton, a CIA agent turned military contractor, Shamsie's novel illustrates the sovereign's agency through highlighting his relations to place and with the Other. This representation of the spy's proxy in Shamsie's novel re-frames the contractor's and the Special Forces Operator's appearance in the post-9/11 American spy fictions, especially with respect to place. Throughout these fictions, the "Culture Talk," which, as I discussed in the previous chapter in relation to the revelatory process, is already endemic to representations of Pashtuns and other groups in Pakistan itself, disperses to become a characteristic of the place itself. As fundamentally dangerous or chaotic or "dark," these places require the restoration of order, enacted via the sovereign and, importantly, another proxy: the drone. Indeed, the American fictions' emphasis on drone usage—almost universally framed as a "good"—represents the extreme exercise of sovereignty: the dehumanization of the Other.

Much like Aslam's novel, *Burnt Shadows* uses historical comparisons to re-situate the centrality of the spy who would be the focus in a conventional rendering of spy fiction. Shamsie's novel revolves around two intertwined families, the Weiss-Burtons and the Tanaka-Ashrafs, who first connect through Konrad Weiss, a German émigré to Japan, and Hiroko Tanaka, a Japanese woman with whom he falls in love. Konrad's killed in the American bombing of Nagasaki in August 1945, and Hiroko, bereft of love and home, travels somewhat waywardly to British India, where Konrad's half-sister, Elizabeth Burton (who is also Ilse Weiss), lives with her British barrister husband, James. Hiroko arrives in Delhi on the eve of the 1947 partition and also meets James's employee, Sajjad Ashraf, an Indian Muslim who becomes Hiroko's Urduwallah and, eventually, her husband as well. This quick description of the characters' entanglements already suggests an historical context: the waning of the British Empire and the ascendance of the American one. *Burnt Shadows* concretizes these overlapping historical trajectories through Henry Burton, James and Ilse's son, who as an adult goes by the name of Harry. Before Hiroko's arrival in India, James and Ilse send Henry off to boarding school in Britain, unintentionally strengthening the boy's attachment to India (Shamsie 2009: 58, 84). Partition marks the departure of the Burtons from India, just as it prevents Sajjad and Hiroko from returning to India after their honeymoon: they are forced to migrate to Karachi (127). While this historical event solidifies Sajjad and Hiroko's joined future—and allows them to raise their son, Raza, as a Pakistani—it hastens James and Ilse's separation. Ilse leaves Britain for New York, and takes her son with her, allowing him to claim his Americanness. Now American, Harry returns to his beloved South Asia as a CIA agent engaged in that agency's covert war in 1980s Afghanistan. He later returns again to the region in the novel's post-9/11 present as a military contractor. Harry's job change, by no means unusual, extra-fictionally speaking, hints at the slippage between the clandestine and citizens' realms, while his abiding attachment to South Asia facilitates the novel's critical points regarding the expansion of sovereignty.

Burnt Shadow's historical long view makes connections between different historical eras—and the players who operate in them—to establish the shifting of sovereignty in a literal sense into a figurative—though more openly violent—one. Hiroko's arrival at the Burton's Delhi home sets the tone. James receives her in his home, located on the other side of the civil lines from Indian Dilli, the entryway of which features his portrait. The narrator shares Hiroko's thoughts on the portrait's accuracy: "she saw that the painting was a good likeness—here was a man at ease with ease" (Shamsie 2009: 43–44). By foregrounding James's comfort in India, Hiroko's initial impression of the Englishman situates him within the broader colonial structure, wherein the British do not question their right to possess India as a colony. These rights of possession extend, the novel suggests, to other white men, too. In a flashback to pre-1940s India, the novel reveals how Konrad "discovered Sajjad" (37) on the streets of Dilli, the old city where few white men ventured. Pointedly, the narrator also shares Ilse's reaction to Konrad's framing of his encounter with the young Sajjad: "'You say that as though he [Sajjad] were a continent'" (37). Ilse's commentary draws a direct line between the white man's privilege or presumed sovereignty, and the colonial project that has bolstered it throughout history. No less possessive or paternalistic—or, perhaps, avun-cular, as Raza takes to calling Harry "uncle," extending the South Asian honorific to the American—Harry's own claiming of sovereignty mirrors that of this earlier generation of colonialists. The novel re-introduces Harry in his American incarnation in a section set in Pakistan, 1982–83. His arrival in Karachi's airport, the narrator explains, prompted Harry to feel the "surge of homecoming that accompanies the world's urban tribes as they enter unfa-miliar landscapes of chaos and possibility" (150). Paradoxical, this char-acterization of Harry's arrival suggests that, as a member of "the world's urban tribes," Harry possesses the power to feel at home in strange places: a suitable definition for the worlding that David from Aslam's novel also experiences. Harleen Singh (2012: 35) labels this power Harry's "effortless reconnaissance of the world," which is itself a manifestation of the "uneven social capital wielded by the characters." The places where this worlding occurs are, notably, "chaotic" but in a way that bears potential, given the proper order. Yet, the novel doesn't allow the idea of strangeness or unfami-liarity to overwhelm Harry. Instead, in the next paragraph, the narrator pointedly marks Harry's possessiveness: "Harry wanted chaos of his cities and nothing less than beauty of his hill towns" (Shamsie 2009: 150). Through claiming places with this singular possessive pronoun, Harry feels "the gnarly stuff of space and time which separated him from his childhood thin to cob-webs" (150). This thinning draws a straight line from James Burton's British colonial ease in India, which characterized Harry's (then Henry's) youth in the region, and Harry's CIA possessiveness of the same places. In these linked historical moments, both father and son experience unfettered privilege.

Harry's role as CIA agent and, later, as PMC ratchets up this privilege, making it into a blatant power over life or, in short, into sovereignty. Believing, at least initially, that Harry is a consular official in Islamabad rather than a CIA agent, Hiroko deems him a "gatekeeper between one nation and the next" (Shamsie 2009: 184). Although mistaken as to the reality of his work, Hiroko's metaphorization of his role does acknowledge Harry's part in distinguishing to whom the law applies and where. The novel illustrates the gatekeeper's power in its ruminations on the American bombing of Hiroshima and Nagasaki, once again using the historical long view to re-situate a dominant perspective and, here, to lend additional insight into Harry's sovereignty. Earlier in the novel as Hiroko and Sajjad get to know one another, she confides to him what her life immediately after the bombing was like. She traveled to Tokyo and worked as a translator for the American occupying force. Aware that this arrangement seems strange, Hiroko explains, "'After the bomb, you might wonder how I could agree to such a thing. But the man who asked me—he had such a gentle face. It was impossible to hold him responsible for what had been done'" (63). Hiroko's explanation for her employment situation highlights an idea of intimacy, as if personal connections automatically nullify or excuse how historical events locate people in relation to one another. As she continues to account for her past, Hiroko then reveals to Sajjad that the gentle-faced American later told her that the bombings "had to be done to save American lives" (63). This naked prioritization of one national type of human life over another recasts the idea of intimacy, allowing national intimacy between strangers to trump intimacy between individuals of different nationalities. Moreover, this prioritization prefigures Harry's role as "gatekeeper," suggesting that Harry's sentimentality, already evidenced in his claiming of place upon arriving in Karachi, may function only as a veneer.

That is, as the passage cited above illustrates, Harry feels the cobwebs distancing his present life from his past one as a child of empire in South Asia "thin" when he flies into Karachi. Notably, Harry's childhood was spent in Delhi and some hill stations; the novel makes no mention of the Burtons traveling to Karachi (and, of course, Islamabad, Harry's Pakistani residence, didn't exist in British India). Yet, Harry flattens these unique locations into one homogenous site over which he can claim possession due at least in part to his childhood memories. With respect to place, sentimentality allows Harry to render place only in terms that relate to him, asserting not just connection but also control. Harry's relation to the people of these places offers an even more striking illustration of his sovereignty. In the novel's present, for example, Harry, now an employee of Arkwright and Glenn, a "private military corporation" (Shamsie 2009: 285), continues to harbor these fond sentiments for South Asia and the "TCNs" (Arkwright and Glenn's acronym for non-CIA, non-contractor, all Third World "Third Country Nationals") that Arkwright and Glenn, itself under contract with the CIA, hires to help run their in-country operations (261). Harry's CIA contact, Steve, calls him out on his sentimentality: "'Harry, Harry, Harry. Wake up and smell the burning buildings. [...] There's too much nostalgia in you. You look at those men [the TCNs] and you see your childhood'" (286). Somewhat crass and certainly biased, Steve's point nonetheless inserts historical exigencies into Harry's sentimentality, which appears to blind him otherwise. The novel forces a reconsideration of Harry's attachment to the place and its people, however, by stressing his conflicting actions. On the one hand, in a show of solidarity, Harry won't wear body armor, because Arkwright and Glenn doesn't provide such protection for the TCNs (308). The corporation's bias also comes out in its theme song, made up by Harry's subordinates, which "rhymed 'Arkwright and

Glenn' with 'dark fighting men'"; none of the Afghan soldiers on the mission sing along (284). On the other, Harry admits to engaging in torture as both a CIA agent and a contractor: "'What wouldn't I do if it was effective? [...] Almost nothing. Children are out of bounds, rape is out of bounds, but otherwise... what works, works'" (289). Implicated in the bias evident in the theme song, Harry's professed attitude toward the use of torture reframes his attempted solidarity with the TCNs into a benevolent sovereignty that only applies where and when Harry sees fit: he can protest Arkwright and Glenn's mistreatment of the TCNs when he wants, and he can torture other Others when he wants, too. Further, Harry's double-sided approach mirrors that of the gentle-faced American who offered Hiroko a job as a translator in Tokyo. Drawing this parallel out means that Harry's desired intimacy with South Asia and its people has its limits, just as the American who hired Hiroko as a translator in post-war Tokyo valued American lives over Japanese ones.

The historically sustained view of Other places as less significant than the US presented by *Burnt Shadows* suggests an abiding if not permanent world-view, wherein the scripts shaping relations between the US and these places are already given. James Burton's bequeath to his son Harry, for instance, extends the former's colonial superiority to the latter in the form of global wars, first the Cold one and, then, the one "on terror." The continuity here hints that neither decolonization nor the fall of communism refigured the exercise of sovereign power by the US over Pakistan or Afghanistan. Moreover, this continuity marks, in Agamben's (2005: 2) terms, "the voluntary creation of a permanent state of emergency (though perhaps not declared in the technical sense) [as] one of the essential practices of contemporary States, including so-called democratic ones."[7] The rendering permanent of the state of exception reinforces the normative process occurring as the clandestine and citizens' realms merge. As Agamben claims, "Insofar as the state of exception is 'willed,' it inaugurates a new juridico-political paradigm in which the norm becomes indistinguishable from the exception" (Agamben 1995: 170). The expansion of the sovereign's power so that, in these fictions, the spy, the contractor, the Special Forces Operator—and not just the sovereign alone—can all suspend the law to preserve it—at least for those not excluded from the order the law establishes—evidences the "willed" aspect of the permanent state of exception, especially given how these figures already possess an affective draw that appears to position their concerns and goals outside of history and politics. My analyses of the post-9/11 American fictions that follow, drawing from the insights gleaned from *Burnt Shadows*, demonstrate this tendency to render permanent the state of exception through the figure of the sovereign and his relation to place.

These American fictions add a trope not explicitly used in Shamsie's novel, however: the drone. In effect the sovereign's appendage, the drone—whether CIA or contractor—further expands the sovereign's power by emphasizing mastery over place in previously unimaginable ways. The question then becomes, what relation does the sovereign and the order he guarantees for some have to the places wherein those excluded from the law of this order live? Both territorialized and non-territorialized considerations are key to any attempt to address this question, and Agamben strives to engage both. If one traces Agamben's thinking about "bare life" and its location in the state of exception, one sees that he starts with the idea of the individual *homo sacer* in "archaic Roman law" (Agamben 1995: 74–111), moves to a contained place—the concentration camp (Agamben 1995: 119–80)—and then considers the radical alteration in how states, including especially democratic ones, now operate (Agamben 2005: 2). Across these examples, the *where* of the state of exception comes into greater focus. Characterizing how states now employ the state of exception, Agamben explains:

> To an order without localization (the state of exception, in which law is suspended) there now corresponds a localization without order (the camp as permanent space of exception). The political system no longer orders forms of life and juridical rules in a determinate space, but instead contains at its very center a *dislocating localization* that exceeds it and into which every form of life and every rule can be virtually taken.
>
> (Agamben 1995: 175, emphasis in original)

Boundaries, national and otherwise, breached, the state of exception, instituted via the sovereign's power, both *dislocates* and *localizes*. In one sense, this doubled and seemingly oxymoronic action opens the possibility that the same place can be experienced differentially, a variability conditioned by who's in and who's out in relation to the law. Additionally, this "*dislocating localization*" creates a problematic (because "out of order") sense of distance from place both for its inhabitants and for those far removed from it. Both these readings encapsulate how the post-9/11 American spy fictions represent the state of exception (without acknowledging it as such, of course). The variability in the experience of place is evident in the urgency to protect Americans from threats inside and outside its borders. Moreover, the prominence of drones in these fictions speaks to the problematic sense of distance accomplished by the "dislocating localization." Drones, here in their fictional representations, marry the invasion attendant to surveillance with the real threat of violence, making the inhabitance of place uncanny. At the same time, drone usage "protects" those who benefit from the order the law establishes in that it keeps these privileged people from danger, extends their reach—or the sovereign's reach extended in their name—and has little care for accountability. Indeed, the American fictions' inclusion of drone usage is one of the prime ways in which the state of exception becomes permanent, even if the actual place of this state of exception shifts.

The acceptability of drone usage in these fictions depends upon the extent to which the protagonist operates as the novel's affective center, since, in most instances, the drones offer cover or back-up for the spy or his proxy. With respect to the American fictions' portrayal of the US and other Americans, the spy and his proxy emphasize the value of the individual, the family, the romantic love narrative in terms that separate these three institutions from their historical conditions of being. In relation to the Other, both in the US and "at the ends of the earth," to cite the subtitle of Mark Mazzetti's (2013c) non-fiction treatment of the CIA's involvement in the "war on terror," the spy and his proxy indulge in "Culture Talk," essentializing and welding together place and people by rendering the results of historical interactions into immutable and ahistorical characteristics. Examples of these characteristics, as framed through "Culture Talk," include reductive and inaccurate portrayals of Islam as violent, of Muslims as fanatical and untrustworthy, and of the places of Islam as chaotic and dangerous, to say nothing of the gendered discourses that insist upon women's oppression at the hands of "brown men." Presumed by "Culture Talk" to exist in these existential conditions, the Other inhabits, whether static or moving, a state of exception, a state of suspended law wherein his relation to this law is as an "outsider" whose existence bolsters the legitimacy of the law. That is, the Other must exist in the state of exception so that those who stand "inside" the law can benefit from the order it produces. The addition of the drone trope in these American proxy-focused fictions extends even further the expansion of sovereignty manifest in the emergence of the spy's proxy in these post-9/11 novels. That is, the drone needs to be a "good guy," as well. Fictive drone usage creates the impression that nothing is outside the US's reach, enhancing the sense of security so crucial to the spy's and the proxy's journey from wounded to wholeness and their positions as sites of authority.

Yet, given the critical space opened by my reading of Shamsie's *Burnt Shadows*, this expansion of sovereignty to include both the spy's proxies and drones approaches Agamben's concept of "dislocating localization," rather than assured security, highlighting not just the Other's refracted relation to place but also that of the sovereign's and his beneficiaries. That is, proxies, drone usage, and their acceptability as providers of security crystallize the significance of the state of exception by showing the tenuous and highly politicized nature of peoples' relation to places. *Burnt Shadows* thus calls attention to an illiteracy, effectively challenging the modes of representation that foster acceptability in the first place. By addressing this illiteracy—by encouraging a shallow reading that acknowledges what's right there on the page—my juxtaposition of Shamsie's novel alongside these post-9/11 American spy fictions highlights how these American fictions contribute to the construction and normalization of a specific type of subjectivity recognizable and desirable in the US. Put another way, this juxtaposition challenges the imposition of the state of exception on Other places and peoples.

As proxies, PMCs and Special Forces Operators share many of the spy's features, commonalities that foster the expansion of sovereignty. The fictional contractors and Special Forces Operators, as I've already noted, bear wounds just like the spies I discussed in the previous chapters. The recurrence of this wound imagery functions in the same way: that is, to encourage a "reading in" to the novel, an identification with the protagonist that makes it seem as though his professional mission actually works in service to his need to become whole. By personalizing the fictions' outcomes, which involve international relations and the messiness of historical circumstances, these novels create the sense that the attributes of the personal wholeness the protagonists seek—i.e. the institutions, such as marriage, family, etc., that are wholeness's hallmarks—exist outside of politics and history, as escapes from what the spies and contractors and Special Forces Operators do for a living. That these post-9/11 American espionage novels enact this escape signals an extension of a long tradition within American literature. According to Bruce Robbins (2011), American fiction features such "rituals of retreat" both before and after 9/11. Further, Robbins speculates that this ongoing theme maintains itself through an assumption that the "world outside the borders of the USA is incomprehensible" (1098). Just as the appeal of sentimentality identified in Berlant's work finds a particular expression in the wound imagery and victim's discourse of these spy fictions, so too does the "retreat into domesticity," which continues to function as an apoliticizing, ahistoricizing, but nonetheless normalizing dynamic (Robbins 2011: 1097). The journey from wounded to wholeness made possible most frequently through the invocation of the romantic love narrative promises a belonging and, relatedly, a security that appears apart, or at least protected, from the threats of the "outside" world. Stacy Takacs (2012: 22) adds to this formulation the idea that such security measures also "offe[r] clarity by dividing the world into categories of 'us' and 'them'." These divisions, in turn, operate at the "level of affect," in Takacs's analysis, "propagat[ing] a sense of urgency and anxiety that [lead] audiences to desire extreme action [against the 'them'] as a means of alleviating the perception of pressure" (64–65). Linking the actions of spies, Special Forces Operators, and the "assorted motley crew of 'privateer' military and intelligence contractors that populate the plots of the contemporary thriller" (Holloway 2009: 40) to what Takacs (2012) refers to as the "alleviation of the perception of pleasure," David Holloway coins the phrase "post-9/11 security sublime," which encourages readers to "absor[b] the world view of the war on terror state" (Holloway 2009: 40). These aesthetic effects make the means by which the novels' protagonists prevail enjoyable and their exertion of the sovereign's power pleasurable, marking the reader's position as one in positive relation to the order the sovereign suspends or upholds. Here again we see Agamben's point about inclusion and exclusion in action. Inclusion means experiencing the pleasure of the "post-9/11 security sublime," which Allan Hepburn (2005: 46) describes as a "catharsis result[ing] from the expulsion of otherness, not its integration into a political process." Exclusion reinforces the reductive essentialisms of "Culture Talk" and thus appears as inevitable and/or necessary.

Several post-9/11 American fictions emphasize the indispensability of the contractor or Special Forces Operator, framing the expansion of sovereignty as a necessity. In Colin MacKinnon's *The Contractor,* for instance, Rick

Behringer's role proves crucial, because, from Rick's own privileged perspective, the CIA doesn't "have the people. They can't do this on their own, they don't know how" (MacKinnon 2009: 111). The "this" to which Rick refers is gathering communications intelligence (COMMINT) on the sale of highly enriched uranium by Russians to a Pakistani protégé of A.Q. Khan, the extra-fictional Pakistani nuclear scientist who was imprisoned—and then freed—in Pakistan for selling nuclear secrets. Even among other contractors, Rick emerges as singularly valuable. While in Pakistan on a mission, Rick meets with the CIA Deputy Chief of Mission at the US embassy in Islamabad. The two men come upon another contractor in the embassy restaurant, which prompts the Deputy Chief to comment:

> Believe it or not, DIA's outsourcing HUMINT [human intelligence] now, which is what Talltree [a contractor organization] does. Talltree's run by morons. […] You can laugh at these fuckheads, and we do, but the uniformed guys—Strategic Support Branch, so called—are about as bad. Strategic Support Branch—SSB—Sorry Stupid Bastards, we call them.
> (MacKinnon 2009: 119)

The Deputy Chief of Mission implicitly singles out Rick as different from other contractors and as more competent than government intelligence officers. Rick's uniqueness holds appeal: highly individualized, assured, capable. The novel continues to reinforce Rick's centrality and, simultaneously, the CIA's limitations through a tripartite structure wherein some chapters are told via Rick's first-person narration and others, including those that chronicle the CIA's plan and limitations, come in a detached third-person, omniscient point of view. Rick's sections create the effect that he's competent, nimble, and aware.

Yet, *The Contractor* creates some dissonance by positing Rick as the best man for the job and as officially inappropriate at the same time. MacKinnon's novel frames Rick's role as contractor—or, rather, the CIA's dependence on him—as less than desirable. In several instances, someone from the CIA expresses his/her distrust of contractors: these non-CIA intelligence workers "have their own agendas" (MacKinnon 2009: 40); or they could "just decide not to keep working" (95); or they're simply "a bunch of […] yahoos" (144). The intelligence community's ambivalence over the use of contractors not only foils Rick's exceptionalism, heightening his appeal as *the* man for the job, but it also reflects back on the establishment itself, suggesting that their conventional way of approaching new threats may not get the job done. In effect, this ambivalence makes the argument for the need to expand the spy's sovereignty to Rick. The novel's conclusion cements this necessity. After Rick helps prevent the sale of the highly enriched uranium, the third-person narrative voice reveals that the CIA's extensive reliance on Rick was illegal. Mike Fiscarelli, Rick's CIA contact, "disobeyed direct orders from the Director of Central Intelligence and the Director of the National Clandestine

Service not to employ such contractors in certain clearly defined geographic areas" (289). Fiscarelli gets around the tangle by classifying all materials related to Rick's mission as "TOP SECRET GOLD" and "TOP SECRET DRAGON," thereby ensuring that no one will discover his use of Rick (289–90). This easy fix, facilitated by the fact that Fiscarelli "has the unilateral power to classify documents in his area of operation, and his actions are not subject to routine review" (289), illustrates the bestowal of sovereign powers upon Rick, for he operates both within and outside of the rules, just as CIA agents do. At the same time that Rick's mission has him in places such as Pakistan and other "certain clearly defined geographic areas" whose access is otherwise restricted grants Rick access to places wherein he can exercise his sovereign power. That is, Rick's relation to place plays out in terms of the state of exception, which he can impose at will. MacKinnon's novel uses the CIA's reticence over using Rick as a device to enhance his appeal and to argue the necessity of his role, especially in places like Pakistan, suggesting that Pakistan somehow needs to be brought under the sovereign's—i.e. Rick's—power.

The representation of the spy's proxy in other post-9/11 American espionage novels presents the use of the spy's proxy in significantly more positive terms and to the same end: the expansion of sovereignty. Dewey Andreas, former Delta and hero of Coes's *Coup d'État*, embodies individualism to an even greater extreme than does MacKinnon's Rick. Dewey's task is to remove a radical cleric who is Pakistan's democratically elected President, because Pakistan has dropped a nuclear bomb on India. The US gets involved in an effort to prevent India from retaliating in kind, which would drag the US into a nuclear stand-off of its own with China, according to the novel's calculus. However, first, the US President and his intelligence team, including Jessica Tanzer, National Security Advisor and Dewey's sometime lover, must find Dewey in Australia, where he's retreated under threat from a "terrorist" billionaire. The novel insists on Dewey's value, thereby justifying this needle in a haystack search in the outback. Through a third-person narrator, readers learn of Dewey's recollections, including of his time "training to be Delta." The lesson Dewey wants to share from his training is not that "being Delta had to do with what you were capable of doing with a weapon and a team. It was the opposite: being Delta was about what you did when you had nothing" (Coes 2011: 39). This idea of hard scrabble survival fits into a broader narrative of American rugged individualism, as well as Dewey's own bent on victim's discourse, which involves his paring down to near nothingness—a new life in Australia as a ranch hand—because he's being hunted by a "terrorist." Dewey isn't really without anything, however, for, as the novel's plot kicks into gear, readers learn that Dewey is, in the words of Coes's fictional CIA Director, "'The one person alive who would make [their plan to remove Pakistan's democratically elected leader], well, maybe a little less than a Hail Mary'" (184). Beyond Dewey's extraordinary skill set, he's a patriot, a must-have characteristic, according to the Director, "'[b]ecause when the shit hits the fan, [Dewey] need[s] to be willing to die for [the] cause. And that's the bottom line'" (184). With Dewey's patriotism foregrounded, *Coup d'État* positions this Delta soldier as above petty politics, as faithful to an unimpugnable ideal, which, consequently, raises his actions in service to this ideal to an unimpugnable level as well. Dewey's central role in the coup that deposes the democratically elected leader and installs a military dictator in his place shows in bold relief how he exercises a sovereign's power—and it's for the "good" of the world.

For the "good" of the world, that is, if the world does not include the "crowds [who support the elected leader] that spread out as far as you could see, in every direction" around the Pakistani President's residence in Islamabad (Coes 2011: 341). Having established Dewey as patriotically unassailable, the novel then conveys his actions as if they, too, are unquestionably "good." Yet, cracks emerge, especially when *Coup d'État* sits alongside a novel such as Shamsie's *Burnt Shadows*. Harry's desire to hold on to South Asia as his ideal of "home" parallels Dewey's idealistic patriotism. For Harry, this ideal of "home" carries over old colonial hierarchies into new globalized relations between the US, Pakistan, and Afghanistan. Dewey's idealistic patriotism similarly hierarchizes place. For example, Dewey staunchly defends the US's right to enact this regime change solely in the name of US priorities and security. As he briefs the general the US is installing to lead Pakistan, for instance, Dewey explains pointedly:

> "The reason you're here right now, and not lying on the ground with a hole in your head, is because of America. [...]
> I'm here because America doesn't feel like fighting a war with China. Get it? You, Pakistan, even India for that matter, you're all a sideshow."
> (Coes 2011: 318)

With an explicit proclamation of his sovereign power, which decides who lives and how, Dewey diminishes the tensions between Pakistan and India that have already resulted in thousands and thousands of deaths in favor of what America wants. Nowhere does Dewey give any consideration to the contradiction that his patriotism is an espousal of a love of democracy while it is also a vehicle by which he squashes an Other people's love of democracy.

Dewey's figurative illiteracy is evident in another scene related to the coup. He and one of his two teammates, a young Pakistani-American renamed Millar, gain access to the Pakistani presidential palace, along with the general they'll be installing as that nation's new leader. The palace is surrounded by crowds chanting in support of their democratically elected leader's actions against India (the crowd doesn't yet know of the coup). The narrator shares that Dewey finds the crowd "overwhelming" (Coes 2011: 340), so much so that he turns to Millar, his subordinate on this mission, and says, "'I wouldn't want to be a pasty-skinned American when those crazy fuckheads'—he nodded to the window—'find out their messiah is gone'" (341). By characterizing the elected Pakistani President as a "messiah," Dewey immediately indicates that he reads Pakistani politics in terms of religion rather than democracy. Further, Dewey's derogatory reference to the Pakistanis supporting their elected government overlooks the obvious: Millar is no "pasty-skinned American." Indeed, the narrator offers Millar's non-verbal reply to Dewey's remark: "Millar stared at Dewey, a hint of concern on his face. Dewey looked away and kept walking up the stairs" (341). An ambiguous bodily response, for certain, as Millar may be staring at Dewey because he's concerned about the crowd, too. Or, Millar could be staring at Dewey, "a hint of concern on his face," because he's just now realizing what he's been a part of: rendering Pakistan into a state of exception. Dewey's averted gaze and wordless exit from the scene—and toward the room where they'll announce the coup—signals the now ineluctable institution of the state of exception. This fine fissure, made evident in Millar's ambiguous reaction to Dewey, mirrors the aforementioned subtle interruption the TCNs in Shamsie's novel effect by remaining silent as the contractors working for Arkwright and Glenn sing their company's theme song (Shamsie 2009: 284). Just as Millar remains silent, the Afghan nationals working with these singing men, "followed more quietly" (284). The narrator's inclusion of this silence effectively speaks the contractors' illiteracy, just as Millar's silence highlights Dewey's.

Such hierarchized visions of place and the people who inhabit them structure the sovereign's power. Indeed, the sovereign can only act as sovereign in relation to places and peoples, for his power requires an object. In the previous chapter, I argued that David Town, the CIA agent in Nadeem Aslam's *The Wasted Vigil*, engages in worlding, wherein he makes Pakistan and Afghanistan into places where he feels at home. Harry's nostalgia, featured in Shamsie's *Burnt Shadows*, operates in the same way. These novels' portrayal of their CIA agents' relations to place alongside other characters' differing relations highlights how David's and Harry's occupation and views of place entail a sense of "power over." By allowing these portrayals to take the lead, so to speak, my analyses of the sovereign's relation to place in the post-9/11 American fictions focus on how they present regions throughout Pakistan and Afghanistan as chaotic, primitive, lawless, etc., thereby offering a justification for the establishment of a state of exception by the spy or his proxy. The expansion of "Culture Talk" to encompass all aspects of place is a primary method by which these novels fix Other locations at the lower end of the hierarchy.

Across the American spy fictions, there is a slippage from the essentialization of a people to an all-out essentialization of place. Standard instances of "Culture Talk," Mamdani's (2004) shorthand phrase for the type of essentialization I mean, involve proclamations of Pakistani mendacity. In Ignatius's *Blood Money* (2011), for example, Cyril Hoffman, CIA Associate Deputy Director, declares, "'The Pakistanis, in my experience, are habitual liars. They are so aggrieved by past slights that they think that any sort of behavior is acceptable'" (Ignatius 2011: 148). Though tipping his hat to history through the mention of "past slights," Hoffman actually invokes historical circumstance as merely an excuse Pakistanis use to give free rein to their "habitual," inherent tendencies. Later, Ignatius's third-person narrator provides a glimpse into Hoffman's thoughts as the CIA Associate Deputy Director reminds himself "to be tolerant [...] if the Pakistani general [who heads Inter-Services Intelligence] said something that he knew to be a lie; it was a matter of cultural dissonance" (218). This passage directly identifies lying as a part of Pakistani culture, some sort of "difference" the American simply needs to deal with. Colin MacKinnon's *Morning Spy, Evening Spy* (2006) makes use of the same trope by having Carl Lindquist, CIA Station Chief in Islamabad, conclude, "'The Paks are just being Paks—who knows why they do anything?'" (MacKinnon 2006: 117). Fed up with the difficulties of dealing with the "Paks," Lindquist goes on to say, "'I'm just one lonely guy out here at the end of the earth shoveling shit for democracy'" (117). Lindquist's comments enact a progression from people to place: "Paks" are frustrating, untrustworthy, and the place in which they live is the "end of the earth," a shitty place where lonely heroes like himself try to dig these poor slobs out from under their own excrement. According to this abiding trope, Pakistanis' inherent untrustworthiness soils their place, too. The abject abides. In Dalton Fury's *Black Site*, for instance, Kolt Raynor, former Delta soldier who now works for a PMC, deliberately refuses to shower before going "in country" for his mission:

> Raynor was filthy. Someone had mentioned that morning that he had refused to shower, refused to eat American-style food in the time between the end of his first training evolution and the beginning of the operation. He wanted to stay dirty; he wanted his insides as well as his outsides to fit into the Pakistan border region where he would be operating.
>
> (Fury 2012: 89)

The American Special Forces Operator must debase himself—inside and out—to "fit into" Pakistan, a clear indication of his own and the novel's view of the place wherein Kolt will, in short order, exercise his sovereign's power.

Kolt's view of place permeates Fury's entire novel. Toward the conclusion, the narrator, favoring a contractor's perspective, marvels, "It was amazing how accustomed people around here [at the Pakistan–Afghanistan border] had become to violence" (Fury 2012: 321). Absent from this observation is any accounting for why violence returns time and again to this border region or for how the contractor's presence there may be contributing to this violence. Instead, the novel portrays this place as mired irrevocably in violence, allowing Pete Grauer, owner of Radiance Security, a private military contracting firm, to deem the region "the Wild West" (100). In this context, Grauer's company's name bears a lot of symbolic purchase: these contractors bring radiance, light, to the "dark corners" of the world. At the same time, the historical referent of Grauer's comment—the American West—also illustrates how Radiance Security takes ownership of place, too. Identifying the appearance of this specific historical theme in post-9/11 American fiction as "tantamount to a reworking of Manifest Destiny," Richard Crownshaw (2011: 772) argues, "The dispossession of other peoples from their lands became the means by which Americans could reoccupy their own land from which they had been dislocated by the attacks of 9/11." In Crownshaw's telling, the fictionalization of post-9/11 America, which would, of course, encompass the espionage fictions I analyze, counters the "dislocating localization" enacted by the attacks of 11 September 2001 with actions in kind. That is, Americans need to re-assert their sovereignty over their own place by (re-)asserting their sovereignty over Others through dispossessing them of their land. Thus, while Manifest Destiny, a mainstay of US history, was originally about domesticating the North American continent, it also reappears, post-9/11, as an example of the necessary imposition of the state of exception elsewhere. Representations of places such as Pakistan and Afghanistan as debased justifies the expansion of American sovereignty, and this expansion gets readily integrated into already dominant American narratives, such as Manifest Destiny, illustrating the US's abiding tropical packaging of the state of exception.

In a similar vein, Michael Gruber's *The Good Son* frames Pakistan and Afghanistan as a "shit hole," laying the groundwork for the imposition of the state of exception (Gruber 2010: 287). This novel features two protagonists: Sonia, a CIA asset, and her son, Theo, a former mujahideen and now a Special Operations soldier in the US Army. The chapters that foreground Theo are told through his first-person perspective, while those chronicling Sonia's kidnapping and incarceration by Islamist radicals are told by a third-person, omniscient voice. Desperate to save his mother, Theo, with the help of his father and extended family in Pakistan, devise an elaborate scheme intended to make the US government think that these Islamist radicals are manufacturing nuclear weapons. Theo's logic is that if the US falls for the ruse, they'll send him, an elite warrior, into Pakistan to diffuse the situation. The plan works, of course, and, inadvertently, Theo does indeed stumble upon Islamist radicals manufacturing nuclear weapons. He also saves his mom. Along the way, Theo engages with former colleagues who have since joined "Force Eight," a private military contracting firm. Pointedly, these PMCs set up an order in Afghanistan from which they benefit:

> Force Eight had leased a big guesthouse in Shari Haw, near downtown Kabul, and fixed it up with new plumbing, air-conditioning, fresh paint, the works. They had their own generator, you could have pizza and hamburgers delivered if you wanted, and the feel of the place was like you were in a pretty good motel in Arizona. They had a big room downstairs with a fifty-inch plasma TV with a satellite feed, lounge chairs, a pool table, and a bar.
>
> (Gruber 2010: 287)

Force Eight's Afghan accommodations replicate suburban America, ensuring a level of comfort and convenience likely unknown to the Afghan "masses." Upon first seeing Theo, the Force Eight contractors get uneasy, until Theo's former Special Operations friend tells them that he's "'a regular white guy in disguise'" (Gruber 2010: 287). While only partially true given that Theo is half Pakistani and perpetrating a ruse on the US government and its employees, including these contractors, the presentation of Theo as a "regular white guy," a description which makes his entrée into Force Eight's accommodations okay, marks the limit of who benefits from the order Force Eight enforces. In the same scene, Theo's friend boasts of the power he exercises: "'Kind of funny, a place occupied by the U.S. Army and they have to hire private guards to watch our people, but there it is. And, by the way, no fucking rules of engagement, either. Someone gets in our face, we waste them and nobody says boo [...]'" (287). The US occupation effectively expands the sovereign's power over place to include Force Eight, and, like Rick in MacKinnon's *The Contractor*, these contractors operate according to rules they both set and enforce. The result is a random violence that plays out on anyone who "gets in [their] face." The order that safeguards Force Eight's comfort and convenience also renders this place—Kabul—into a state of exception, wherein laws are suspended in order to differentiate individuals' relation to the law. In other words, the randomness of Force Eight's rules create the disorienting effects of "dislocating localization."

The inclusion of drones in these post-9/11 American spy fictions develops further the disorienting effects of Agamben's "dislocating localization," extending the spy's sovereignty through not only to his proxy but also to this remote-controlled killing device. As metaphor, these fictionalized drones demonstrate the inescapable reach of the sovereign, as well as his ability to transform any location into a state of exception. As literary manifestations of extra-fictional realities, the drones featured in these novels extend Agamben's notion of "dislocating localization." As Gabriel Giorgi and Karen Pinkus assert, Agamben's "dislocating localization" marks a "containment [that] cannot confine in space what is a *general* biopolitical condition" (Giorgi and Pinkus 2006: 104, emphasis in original). In other words, no place is singularly secure or protected but rather permeable and, depending on perspective, vulnerable to becoming a state of exception. The entrée of the contractor and the Special Forces Operator signals one kind of permeability: that between the clandestine and citizens' realms. Drones represent another kind of permeability, wherein the citizen isn't necessarily made more vulnerable but is made aware of a vulnerability that has always existed. With this awareness comes the understanding that those who benefit from the order supported by the sovereign's power might just as readily suffer from being abandoned by the law's protection.

Several of the American fictions I've been discussing deploy drones, and they represent drone usage along a spectrum that valorizes and anthropomorphizes the machines, at one end, and suggests the ways the devices heighten vulnerability, at the other. In other words, these depictions range from the familial to the uncanny or unnerving. Such a broad variety suggests the methods with which the novels, as cultural productions, endow drones with meaning and render this meaning acceptable. In Fury's *Black Site*, for instance, drones occupy several roles, including as babies, heroes, and predators. To their pilot, Pam Archer, formerly of the US Air Force and now a member of Radiance Security, the drones are Baby Boy and Baby Girl (Fury 2012: 88). Pam develops a strong attachment to the two machines—stronger than permitted her in the Air Force—simply because she's in close proximity with "her birds"; so close, in fact, that "sometimes she *did* touch them. She couldn't help it. They were beautiful, and they were hers" (87). This concertedly familial, even maternal presentation of a pilot's connection to the drones reinforces the idea that the machines are extensions of the contractor's sovereignty. At the same time, by labeling the unmanned planes Pam's babies, the novel also domesticates them, tames or exerts control over the violence they can wreak. In a sense, this sentimental portrayal of Pam's connection with the drones neutralizes the planes' destructive capabilities, at least with respect to the people for whom Radiance works—i.e. the US. At the novel's conclusion, however, Baby Boy morphs into what Kolt calls "A kamikaze Predator" as Pam uses the drone as a "huge kinetic missile" that slams into two truckloads of Taliban soldiers who are after Kolt near the Pakistan–Afghanistan border (335, 334). Figuratively, Pam sacrifices her "son" for Kolt, who himself represents America as a former Delta soldier. At the same time, Pam exerts her sovereign power by defying orders that forbid her from destroying the Predator, her most egregious offense, as far as her boss is concerned, and by breaching Pakistan's own sovereignty in order to kill the men pursuing Kolt. Pam's stunt does save Kolt, though, and for that her boss praises her: "'That was incredible. Nice work'" (336). From the personalized relationship between Pam and her babies to the violation of another nation's sovereignty, *Black Site*'s representation of drone usage valorizes the detached control over place and people these machines make possible. Such representations reassure those who benefit from the order the sovereign upholds. Apparently, these beneficiaries are securely located.

Coup d'État's use of drones functions in a similar manner to reassure beneficiaries. One of the novel's final scenes features Jessica Tanzer, the National Security Advisor and Dewey's lover, directing a drone pilot on a mission to bomb the very military dictator Dewey just installed in Pakistan. This operation is a revenge mission, as this dictator double-crossed Dewey. Jessica rights a personal wrong, which proves emotionally satisfying, as she orders yet another breach of Pakistani sovereignty—both through the use of the drone and through the assassination of another of that nation's leaders, howsoever artificially installed. Jessica has the dictator on the phone even as she's lining up the drone strike. As Jessica taunts the dictator over his perfidy, she "mov[es] her left middle finger to the red button atop the joystick" used to pilot the drone (Coes 2011: 456). Just as the dictator rises to her taunts, Jessica tells him, "'Look up in the sky. [...] That's America flying over your head'" (457). Button depressed, dictator vanquished, and Jessica is hardly phased; instead, she "patted the UAV [unmanned aerial vehicle] pilot on the back, then reached for her Louis Vuitton briefcase, picked it up, and stepped toward the door" (457). Like Fury's novel, this representation of drone usage originates in the personal realm and also bears with it strong jingoistic strains—"That's America flying over your head"—which demonstrate the sovereign's seemingly limitless reach. With these recurring tropes, Coes's novel also shows how the beneficiaries of the sovereign's power experience a different exceptionalism at the same time that those afflicted with "bare life" exist in the vulnerable state of exception. That is, pointedly, the narrator identifies Jessica's Louis Vuitton briefcase. Such an extravagant accessory effectively "brands" American sovereignty as an "it" bag, tying conspicuous consumerism explicitly to American sovereignty. This product placement thus clearly signifies Jessica's success, her chosenness, which, in part, appears to qualify her to toy with the leader of Pakistan before she personally, though remotely, eviscerates him. The Louis Vuitton reference alters what *Coup d'État*'s use of the drone means: whereas Pam's maternal attachments to Baby Boy and Baby Girl softened the drones' literal and figurative power, Jessica's direct personal involvement—her phone call to the dictator, her pressing of the button—creates a sense of hardness or toughness, well earned and well rewarded, as if the Protestant work ethic re-emerges, post-9/11. Reassurance does not come as readily in this second portrayal, and this exercise of the sovereign's power raises the stakes significantly, as those banned from the law aren't nameless, faceless extremists, but an individuated, powerful character who acts as a sovereign in his own right.

MacKinnon's *The Contractor* depicts drones as the most detached from both their operators and their "prey." As the CIA and other American intelligence agencies close in on the Russians and Pakistanis engaged in the sale and purchase of highly enriched uranium, these agencies depend upon drones to track and kill the "bad guys." The novel amasses a litany of acronyms in its description of who is "present" to watch the drones do their work:

> The Director of Central Intelligence, three of his deputies including the Director of the National Clandestine Service and five other NCS officers are in the OPCOM/NPTG Operations Center, fifth floor. [...]
>   They are watching three large flat-panel displays showing the identical image of pale, rose-pink land, the desert south of Dubai, slipping beneath the belly-mounted camera of an MQ-9 Predator. The Predator is armed with six Hellfire AGM-114 air-to-ground, laser-guided missiles.
>
> (MacKinnon 2009: 280)

On the one hand, the use of acronyms and the indulgence in details appear to lend credibility to the fictional situation. On the other, though, such a presentation also distances readers; in comparison to the other two examples I've already discussed, there is no personal connection here to the pilots or the important figures assembled. The narrator then reveals that one drone pilot is at "Nellis AFB, Las Vegas, Nevada," and the other, "Central Command HQ, in Doha, Qatar[,] in the Persian Gulf" (MacKinnon 2009: 280). The pilots' distance from each other cancels out the possibility of camaraderie between them. No brothers in arms, here, at least in the novel's portrayal. Compounding this clinical representation, the third-person narrator comments, when the pilot based at Nellis speaks, that "[h]e has no accent" (281). Beyond also being identified as a young man, this pilot's lack of accent is the only defining detail the narrator shares. Yet, that is no definition at all, as the pilot's unaccented speech frustrates any ability to "locate" him dialectally. In a sense, this pilot, whose reach is everywhere, is nowhere at all. Thus, figuratively, he embodies a free-ranging power to surveil and kill without ever making himself known or seen. Less reassuring, less familiar, MacKinnon's representation of drones in *The Contractor* unnerves because it dislocates relation to place: the drone pilot as the sovereign's proxy is absent yet omnipresent, and this ephemerality in its unknowability—who is sovereign? where is he?—un-eases everyone's relation to place.

The sovereign's relation to place, i.e. the creation of the state of exception, has been central to my analyses of the emergence of the spy's proxy in these post-9/11 fictions. At base, I've argued that the spy's proxy makes explicit the merging of the clandestine and citizens' realms, which at the same time blurs the distinction between violence and the law, to echo Agamben's concerns. Even more, the blurring of this distinction serves, according to Agamben, as an example of the "society of the spectacle." This emphasis on the visible resonates with my interest in reading the Pakistani appropriation of spy fiction conventions as a type of "propaganda by deed." Shamsie's novel performs this function, as it exhibits in plain sight what's at stake in Harry's claiming of place both when he is a CIA agent and, later, a private military contractor. In this latter role, Harry possesses many of the same characteristics as the spy, including an ability to act as sovereign, an ability that shapes his relation to place. This novel's concentrated portrayal of Harry as proxy helps identify the illiteracies operating in the American fictions, wherein the proxy also acts as sovereign by rendering the place of the Other into a state of exception and relegating the Other himself to "bare life." In the next chapter, I explore further this notion of abandonment through the figure of the "terrorist," with a particular interest in how this figure relates to those protected by the law and to the sovereign himself.

Notes

1 Agamben directs this point explicitly at Foucault's work in *The History of Sexuality*. Indeed, much of Agamben's thinking in *Homo Sacer* aims to "correct" or "complete" Foucault's thought (Agamben 1995: 8), which, for Agamben, does not sufficiently address the "zone of indistinction (or, at least, the point of

intersection)" at which Foucault's biopolitical model encounters or experiences "objective power" (5–6).

2 See the end of *State of Exception* for Agamben's formulation of how change may happen (Agamben 2005: 88). Leland de la Durantaye (2009: 234–38) also addresses the critical response to Agamben's seemingly constrictive formalism.

3 I pursue this banned existence at greater length in the next chapter.

4 De la Durantaye (2009: 223) explains how Agamben's "paradigm" may be of use in various situations despite its lack of historical specificity: "[T]o be genuinely illuminating Agamben's paradigms must strike an exceptionally delicate balance between respect for the uniqueness of historical phenomena and the use to be made of those phenomena for understanding *other* situations." For his own part, Agamben presents himself as "'working historically,' but not as a historian" (quoted in de la Durantaye 2009: 224). Malini Johar Schueller (2009: 241) takes issue, as have others, with Agamben's methodology, identifying it as a "universal" deployed knowingly in critique of a "clearly imperial moment." Although I do not make use of Agamben's turn to the figure of the Muselman, which he borrows from Primo Levi, Schueller sees this move in Agamben's *Homo Sacer* series as the most urgent site at which postcolonialists must pose questions about Agamben's "paradigm" (243–46).

5 Agamben turns to concentration camps and, more recently, cities as examples of states of exception. This expansion supports my point regarding how post-9/11 espionage fictions frame certain places as similar "zones of indistinction." See de la Durantaye (2009), especially pages 219–23, for a thorough review of critical responses from the likes of Antonio Negri and Ernesto Laclau, among others, to Agamben's use of the concentration camp.

6 Agamben makes this observation upon identifying the state of exception as a topographical figure, such as the concentration camp or the city.

7 Although Agamben (2005: 1–3) uses the phrase "state of emergency" in this quote, he is discussing the permanent institution of the state of exception in the larger passage.

4 "Terrorist"

The US government's Department of Homeland Security holds a trademark for their "If You See Something, Say Something™" campaign. Their website promotes the campaign via subheadings that include, "Homeland Security begins with Hometown Security." Rhetorically, the department's name and its campaign shape what "terrorism or terrorism-related crime" mean in the US ("If You See Something"). Donald Pease makes explicit the ideological work that the phrase "homeland security" does, arguing that the "*Homeland Security Act* [...] engendered an imaginary scenario wherein the national people were encouraged to consider themselves dislocated from their country of origin [the US] by foreign aggressors [...]" (Pease 2006: 75, emphasis in original). Through the production of the sense of dislocation, "homeland security" works to localize within national borders a militancy against the Other, as Amy Kaplan (2003: 87) notes. The addition of "hometown security" arguably exacerbates that lingering sense and ongoing fear of dislocation, illustrating Agamben's idea of "dislocating localization," discussed in the previous chapter, from another perspective. That is, "homeland security" strikes a defensive posture, domestically anyway, which relies on anxiety over or fear of having place itself become strange through terrorist violence. As Sara Ahmed points out, this defensive posture "presume[s] that things are not secure, in and of themselves, in order to justify the imperative *to make things secure*" (Ahmed 2004b: 76, emphasis in original). Efforts to secure "*things*," in Kaplan's view, prompt a desire for homogeneity, a claiming of place in exclusive terms. At the same time, this localization obscures the degree to which post-9/11 US foreign policy extends the imperative of "homeland security" well beyond the homeland's borders, thereby dislocating the Other in other places, too. According to Kaplan:

> A relation exists between securing the homeland against the encroachment of foreign terrorists and enforcing national power abroad. The homeland may contract borders around a fixed space of nation and nativity, but it simultaneously also expands the capacity of the United States to move unilaterally across the borders of other nations.
>
> (Kaplan 2003: 87)

The domestically and internationally oriented impulses of "homeland security" construct a notion of "home" based on fear and containment of those who belong and of the Other alike that is meant to pass as comfort, inviolability, and stability.[1]

Further, as Kaplan and others contend, any notion of a homeland relies upon some place, some people who are identifiably "foreign" to those who benefit from the order the "homeland" provides (Kaplan 2003: 86). James Andreas Manos makes a similar point, concluding that national security is "a project that decides who is embraced by the juridical and the political, and who is denationalized, without country and without rights, and compelled to face the blunt force of the sovereign nation-state" (Manos 2004: 135–36). This two-sided project, Manos contends, "secures the national body" by producing "bodies that are removed from the juridical order in the name of security" (140). In effect, the metamorphosis of the Other into one who inhabits "bare life" coincides with a metamorphosis that enhances or appears to secure the citizen's belonging in the national body. Manos takes this creationism one step farther when he argues that the sovereign decision that results in the state of exception "removes the threatening body at the same time it produces that body" (145). Crucially, this claim requires us to consider from where supposedly inherent tendencies and characteristics come—do they reside in the body of *homo sacer* or do they attach to that body once it's labeled as such?—considerations that form a direct challenge to the power of "Culture Talk." In many ways, then, the very name of the Department of Homeland Security rhetorically encapsulates how the sovereign's relation to place creates those who are included and excluded.

The "If You See Something, Say Something™" campaign develops the department's rhetorical power in other ways, as well. A federally registered trademark makes the trademarked material into a brand. As a slogan that facilitates the dislocating localizations discussed above, "If You See Something, Say Something™" effectively brands the US as a regularized state of exception with respect to both its domestic and international policies, as I discussed in the previous chapter. This slogan is also germane to this chapter's focus on the "terrorist." Two verbs anchor the campaign's slogan: "see" and "say." With respect to the visual, the campaign instructs Americans: "Factors such as race, ethnicity, national origin, or religious affiliation alone are not suspicious" ("If You See Something"). "Alone," the sentence's lone qualifier, leaves enough semantic and visual space for the modifiers "race, ethnicity, national origin, or religious affiliation" to provide some reason to be suspicious. This string of modifiers also links and likens concepts that don't necessarily stand in any relation to one another, accomplishing the metonymic work Ahmed sees operating throughout post-9/11 American representations of the "war on terror." Ahmed (2004b: 76) argues that "the slide of metonymy can function as an implicit argument about the causal relations between terms [...], but in such a way that it does not require an explicit statement." Such a slide occurs here both metonymically and syntactically to heighten suspicion of the

Other based on categories that only signify because they are historically overdetermined. "Race," for instance, often serves as a visual category, something people think can be determined by sight (or want to determine by sight, right on the surface of the body), while "national origin or religious affiliation" cannot be concluded just by how someone looks. "Ethnicity" only complicates the implications of this list of words, since "ethnicity" frequently stands in for "race," even while it can be an adopted trait insofar as a person can take on the cultural characteristics of another "ethnicity"—or nation or religion, for that matter—due to any number of circumstances. Yet, as Ahmed (2004b: 63) also contends, certain bodies become fearsome to certain other bodies due to "past histories of association" between those bodies and between the terms used to represent those bodies. By having these terms all appear together as potentially giving reason (to whom?) to be suspicious, these words invite the collapse of categorizing constructs onto the body itself. The body of the suspicious person, thus, becomes a text to be read by those who belong in the "homeland."

"Say," the second verb of the "If You See Something, Say Something™" slogan, follows both logically and imperatively from the visual component of this loose conditional sentence. If the body of the suspicious person does indeed become the text read by those who belong, then this campaign asks Americans to read the body's surface, to apprehend via overdetermined visual clues rather than through exploration or consideration. Significantly, this reading of the body's surface is not the same as shallow reading. The metaphorization of "propaganda by deed" that I've been developing throughout the preceding chapters insists upon visuality as communication, to be sure, but in such as way as to call attention to illiterate or poorly read understandings of what can be seen. In other words, the "If You See Something, Say Something™" campaign operates as an illiteracy. My own interest in a shallow reading methodology means to spotlight precisely how this reading of the "terrorist's" body is already at work—but infrequently examined—in so many fictional and extra-fictional situations dealing with terrorism and the state of exception. What's being said after what's been seen becomes crucial, for the "said" serves as an explanation of the "terrorist's" motivation, the act's meaning, and the US's relation to these matters. In other words, the "said" expresses a knowledge claim; in these post-9/11 American fictions, it represents a crucial element in or the culmination of the revelatory process discussed in Chapter 2. In that sense, the "said" contributes to the spy's or the proxy's affective appeal, because it endows him with a knowingness that lends credibility and a sense of security. Further, as I've been discussing, the revelatory process contributes to the persuasive weight of "Culture Talk," thereby helping make the spy's or proxy's exercise of sovereign power acceptable, which means it also works to frame the "terrorist" as the one who's banned from the law, who inhabits, disadvantageously, the state of exception. Agamben deems the banned person *homo sacer*, one who is "not, in fact, simply set outside the law and made indifferent to it but rather *abandoned* by it, that is, exposed and threatened on the threshold in which life and law, outside and inside, become indistinguishable" (Agamben 1995: 28–29). *Homo sacer* is stripped of rights, is effectively nationless, but is not "free" from law. Instead, the banned person is vulnerable and can be killed with impunity. This vulnerability comes about because of the banned person's residence in the state of exception, a zone of indistinction wherein the law is suspended in order for the law to be protected. Inversely, the "said" portion of Homeland Security's campaign positions those speaking with the sense that they have mastered or conquered the Other, for they understand what makes "terrorists" tick. In the language I used throughout the previous chapter, those with the power to "say" also share in the sovereign's power, either by offering authoritatively an explanation for the "terrorist" or by benefitting from the law's protection, i.e. by not being abandoned by the law.

In this chapter, I focus on the "seen" and the "said" in order to examine how post-9/11 Pakistani and US fictions represent the figure of the "terrorist." This focus allows me to develop one of the interconnected issues I identified in the Introduction: namely, how the Pakistani texts' appropriation of spy fiction's conventions highlights the logic through which the state of exception becomes acceptable. I use the ambivalence several Pakistani novels employ to portray the suspected "terrorist" to call into question the "knowledge" about "terrorists" produced by the explanations offered in the US fictions. Framed in the Department of Homeland Security's campaign, my analyses concentrate, first, on the "seen." H.M. Naqvi's *Home Boy* (2009) and Mohsin Hamid's *The Reluctant Fundamentalist* (2007) both complicate the sovereign's relegation of the excluded to "bare life" by foregrounding how the "terrorist's" body— which is "seen"—stands in relation to the law. In doing so, these Pakistani fictions individuate without psychologizing and, thus, encourage a recognition of circumstance rather than abstraction or universalization. The "said" provides the framework for the second part of my analyses. With the ambivalence featured in the Pakistani novels in mind, I contrast the certainty with which the American fictions "know" the "terrorist." Of particular interest here is how these explanations make use of tropes derived from "Culture Talk" and how these tropes then justify the relegation of the "terrorist" to the state of exception.

Naqvi's *Home Boy* and Hamid's *The Reluctant Fundamentalist* hone readers' literacy in the sense that these Pakistani fictions construct the figure of the alleged "terrorist" as an exploration of "bare life." The perspective of one excluded from the law but still made an object of it promotes an indeterminacy that addresses what Jeffory Clymer (2003: 218) sees as "a paucity of non-absolutist tropes with which to understand each other." That is, Naqvi's and Hamid's novels focus on the alleged "terrorist's" body to highlight the inscriptions these bodies bare and, in so doing, refuse to shunt these figures into discrete, knowable categories. This refusal matters in at least three ways: first, such representations of the alleged "terrorist" mark the commonalities shared by those included in and those excluded by the law, showing how all subjects' relationship to the law is radically contingent; second, these fictions' refusals help develop an idea of resistance many critics see lacking in theoretical discussions of "bare life"; and, third, such refusals complicate the post-9/11 American spy fictions' penchant for explanation, which amounts to a claim of mastery over the Other.

Of the Pakistani fictions I've been discussing, Naqvi's *Home Boy* appears the least like a conventional espionage novel. Instead, the novel comes off as a story of three Pakistani friends experiencing New York City pre- and post-9/11. Yet, the novel's tracking of the changes in the city and the friends' belonging to it across that pre-/post- divide illustrates the effects of the sovereign decision that renders life for *some* who suddenly become suspicious into a highly visible condition of "bare life." As the friends experience this change in their own bodies, they find themselves enmeshed in the net cast by the US security state, which brings them into contact with federal agents who wield a sovereign's power over them. Chuck, the novel's narrator, is a Pakistani national who comes to the US for university. Upon his arrival, in the novel's past, Chuck, whose actual name is Shehzad, links into the extensive Pakistani-American community in New York City, a network that eventually allows him to befriend AC (Ali Chaudhry), an immigrant seeking US citizenship, and Jimbo (Jamshed), who is a natural born American citizen of Pakistani descent. Each character's citizenship status matters, because it marks their relation to the state, though, as the novel plays out, these relationships, which go from "guest" to full-fledged, rights-bearing citizen, don't guarantee protection from the sovereign decision. Chuck, AC, and Jimbo feel the full brunt of the sovereign decision, which renders the places they inhabit into states of exception, while on a quest of sorts to find a fourth friend, the Shaman or Mohammed Shah, another Pakistani immigrant who lives in Connecticut and who the novel frames as a Pakistani Jay Gatsby (Naqvi 2009: 27). The three friends break into the Shaman's house and briefly take up residence, which gets disrupted after the neighbors see something and say something to the Federal Bureau of Investigation (FBI). Chuck describes their arrest in terms that emphasize the visual:

> People had come out on their porches in ones and twos, in striped pajamas and robes to gawk at the spectacle: in the coruscating lights of four squad cars and an unmarked sedan arranged in a broad semicircle [...], a congregation of a dozen or so cops talked among themselves in low voices and into radios as a couple of suits paraded by with three disheveled, swarthy men in handcuffs.
>
> (Naqvi 2009: 130)

The entire scene is a "spectacle" to the Connecticut residents, something to be gawked at, and the friends' swarthiness, their very bodies, serve as the spectacle's focal point. While he can, Chuck assesses appearances, too, imagining that the "next-door neighbor" would tell reporters, "*I saw them going in, coming out, and they seemed okay—you know, not from around here—but okay* [...]" (Naqvi 2009: 131, emphasis in original). This glimpse into Chuck's imagination signals how his swarthy Pakistani appearance marks his Otherness, the fact that he's *"not from around here,"* and, thus, prompts the suspicion that purportedly justifies the neighbor's call.

By linking suspicion of terroristic intent to Chuck and his friends' *"not from around here"* appearance, this scene illustrates what Ahmed calls the "stickiness" of affect, specifically fear. In Ahmed's formulation, fear as a type of affect moves between signs as current circumstances and contexts call upon "past histories of association" (Ahmed 2004b: 66–67, 63). Fear "sticks" to certain signs given how the conditions of the present draw upon the past (66–67). Central to Ahmed's intertwined notions of the movement and stickiness of affect is the claim that "affect does not reside positively in the sign or commodity, but is produced as an effect of its circulation" (45). Thus, in the conflation operating in this arrest scene, post-9/11 discourses fuel suspicions, circulate fear, and then "stick" to likely candidates, such as Chuck, AC, and Jimbo, whose sole motivation is to find out what happened to their friend the Shaman. This stickiness guarantees that each character inhabits a portable state of exception, which travels with him wherever he goes up until the time that the present calls upon a different set of historical associations that will prompt the movement of affect to other signs. This portability, made possible by the very fact that these characters inhabit marked brown bodies, qualifies the liberating potential scholars such as Sedgwick and Frank (1995: 12), as well as Massumi (1996: 224, 228), locate in the body, which, in their formulations, serves as the locus of affect. Moreover, following Ahmed, the fearsomeness attributed to the friends by the neighbors and the federal agents does not exist within them; in other words, Ahmed's theory of affect's circulation challenges the essentialism common to "Culture Talk," reversing arguments for inherent characteristics by locating affective responses within collective dynamics. Such a recognition of the collective circulation of affective response grants further credence to the critical conversation that identifies espionage fiction, among other types of cultural phenomena, as a discourse that helps shape readers' attitudes through affective appeals.

Thoroughly stuck, Chuck, AC, and Jimbo begin their descent into "bare life." Federal agents, some with the FBI, others whose affiliations remain unknown, haul a now-hooded Chuck, AC, and Jimbo to the Metropolitan Detention Center in New York, a place Chuck refers to as "'American's Own Abu Ghraib'" (Naqvi 2009: 133), on suspicion of "terrorist activities" (131, 136). Chuck gets released, Jimbo gets sprung thanks to his white American girl-friend's connection to the governor, and AC remains incarcerated for posses-sion of cocaine, a convenient deus ex machina for the powers that be. In effect, these characters all undergo a "dislocating localization," in which their inhabitancy of the city alters radically in a short period of time, and, while Jimbo is able to "return" to some semblance of his pre-9/11 life, the novel suggests that none of the three friends fully reclaims his body from the conditions of "bare life" to which they are relegated post-9/11.

As I note, the arrest scene hinges upon the visual, illustrating how both the Connecticut residents and Chuck himself are reading the episode. *Home Boy* textually plays with the visual prior to this scene, as well, to illustrate the tendency toward misreading or, in other words, to address the gap in literacy. As Birte Heidemann (2012: 294) argues, "Naqvi's use of malapropisms, puns, language play, syntactic mutilations and slips-of-the-tongue are studded with covert counter-rhetorical tropes that render post-Orientalist signifiers as innately insidious, inimical, if not in(s)ane." Chuck's positions as object or possessor of "bare life" and as narrator allow him to highlight this gap even as he recognizes his inability to surmount it within the novel's fictional universe. The novel plays with the visual through spelling, for instance, a move that allows readers to see the differences between how "Americans" refer to Chuck and his friends and how the friends refer to themselves. The first instance of playful spelling occurs during a bar fight scene. Two white drunks, to whom Chuck refers as "Brawler No. 1" and "Brawler No. 2," accost the friends at one of their usual haunts. "Brawler No. 1 hissed, 'A-*rabs*'" (Naqvi 2009: 30). Noting to himself that this incident is "the first time anything like this had happened to us at all," Chuck understands that, post-9/11, "This was different" (30). Despite Jimbo's insistence that "'[w]e're not the same,'" Brawler No. 2 responds, "'Moslems, Mo-hicans, whatever'" (30). Fists and beer bottles fly shortly after this exchange.[2] Notably, Chuck as narrator transcribes Brawler No. 2's response as "Moslems," even though he repeatedly refers to himself and to his other co-religionists as "Muslims." "Moslem" appears in pre-twentieth-century entries in the *Oxford English Dictionary*, suggesting that this spelling fits into a colonial context. Chuck's use of this spelling in his transcription of Brawler No. 2's dialogue thus invokes an entire worldview, one that asserts dominance over the Other. Visually, this spelling works to locate Chuck and his friends within an historical state of exception: the colony. Chuck's self-referential use of the more standard and contemporary "Muslim" visually challenges that colonial dominance, that sovereign decision, inviting readers to see the differences in how specific words can contain or release individuals. Further, this "Moslem"/"Muslim" incident, the first instance of visual play in the novel, occurs post-9/11, serving as a harbinger of the discursive and material violence soon to be inflicted upon the friends.

Another instance of visual play occurs just before the perp walk scene I describe above. When the FBI agents show up at the Shaman's house, they ask AC and Chuck, "Where's Mr. Mo-Hammid Shaw?" (Naqvi 2009: 126). Chuck's response provides the visual difference: "Well, we hadn't heard from Mohammed for some time, so we thought we'd just, you know, check up on him" (126). This misspelling of names happens on several occasions; Jimbo, whose last name is "Khan" is referred to as "Kahn" (216); Chuck is called "Shay-zad" when his name is "Shehzad" (196). Again, the visual discrepancies point to a broader and more serious misrecognition or mis-reading of these characters' identities. Those in power—the FBI, the hospital staff who mis-refer to Jimbo, and a prospective employer who gets Chuck's name wrong—all misapprehend these Pakistanis, and, significantly, all of these misapprehensions occur post-9/11. Given the specific instances in which these visual plays take place, the novel connects the power of language with the power of violence and control. That is, the use of antiquated spellings and phonetic renderings coincides with moments when the Pakistani friends have no power or control over the situation and, thus, become the objects referred to rather than the subjects who self-determine. At the same time, the novel uses textual differences—e.g. "Moslem" and "Muslim"—to play with the idea that the visual provides certainty. Chuck's narratorial play with how certain words and names appear acknowledges the post-9/11 gap between how the Pakistani characters represent themselves and how "Americans" see them. In other words, the spelling play highlights an illiteracy, and the lesson about who's vulnerable and who's powerful that this play attempts to impart matters more and more as the three friends descend into "bare life."

As character, Chuck knows he's vulnerable nonetheless. Even before his arrest (but after 9/11), Chuck understands how he's "contained" because of his appearance. He's uneasy, for instance, about the prospect of "an expedition deep into the heart of Connecticut" (Naqvi 2009: 50), an uneasiness perhaps borne of that state's metonymic function as a prime site of American privilege. As the three friends start out on their journey, misgivings aside, they get pulled over by the police, an event that makes Chuck think, *"We're a bunch of brown men in a car,* [on] *the night of heightened security in the city"* (97, emphasis in original). This awareness of the spaces Chuck and his friends can't inhabit inverts the worlding apparent in several other novels' representations of the spy. Harry Burton in Kamila Shamsie's *Burnt Shadows* (2009) attempts to re-make contemporary South Asia into the British India of his youth, just as David Town in Nadeem Aslam's *The Wasted Vigil* (2008) claims belonging to the area around Marcus's house by building a bark canoe like the one he had as a boy in North America. These efforts represent the spies' abilities to occupy Other spaces on their own terms. Naqvi's novel narrates the other side of this occupation, showing how Chuck knows his boundedness. Together, this worlding and the inability to do so illustrate Ahmed's point about how fear contains some and liberates others: "It is the regulation of bodies in space through the uneven distribution of fear which allows spaces to become territories, claimed as rights by some bodies and not others" (Ahmed 2004b: 70). Insofar as post-9/11 fears provoke defensive postures in the name of national security, both at home and abroad, they also grant the right to the fearful, i.e. Americans, to expand into spaces. On the other side of this equation, these defensive postures also strip the rights of the fearsome, containing them in space, hence Chuck's awareness of his spatial transgressions.

Containment operates visually, as well. Chuck fixates on being seen. On the subway just after his release from the Metropolitan Detention Center, for instance, Chuck reveals his discomfort:

> I looked away when people looked at me. [...] I was conscious of the way
> I looked, behaved, the way I anxiously scratched my nose, my ear. When
> they announced "Please report any suspicious activity or behavior" over
> the speakers, I closed my eyes like a child attempting to render himself
> invisible.
>
> (Naqvi 2009: 154)

As character, Chuck loses the ability to challenge the visual that he possesses
as narrator and succumbs to—even internalizes—the notion that he is fearsome,
because he's brown-skinned and Muslim. This internalization exemplifies the
portability of the state of exception. Chuck's anxiety escalates to the point
where he has a full-scale panic attack in Central Park. Seated on a bench,
Chuck sees "a short black female cop," and, "[a]lthough there was nothing
unusual in her appearance, nothing threatening in her manner, [he] instinctively
shrank within [himself] and looked away" (Naqvi 2009: 249). This dodge is
merely a prelude to a breakdown during which Chuck loses consciousness
(249). The image of Chuck shrinking within himself marks an extreme:
his experiences as *homo sacer* atrophy his right to occupy even the space of
his own body.

Returning to the arrest scene, Chuck imagines the event as newsworthy
precisely because of the conflation of "swarthy" men with "terrorist," a conflation made all the more significant by the fact that the three friends are
Pakistani and Muslim. While in custody, Chuck realizes the precariousness of
his status, not because he's guilty of "terrorist activities" but simply because
of that conflation coupled with his visa status. A federal agent, who remains
unidentified except for the fact that he reminds Chuck of Mickey Rooney
(Naqvi 2009: 132), begins Chuck's interrogation by asking him "'how d'you
feel about what happened on September eleventh?'" (135). Assessing the
question as "ridiculous," Chuck replies, "'I want to make my phone call. I
know my rights'" (135). The agent "fired back": "'You aren't American! [...]
You got no fucking rights'" (135). This interrogator, along with a second
whom Chuck refers to as "Grizzly" (143), never reveal their real names or for
which federal agency they work. This anonymity matters, because it heightens
the sense that the state itself degrades Chuck, while it also suggests that
anyone could wield this power over him. That is, the sovereign is interchangeable, an expansion already evident in the post-9/11 US fictions via the
spy's proxies. In Naqvi's novel these two interrogators fill in, then, as yet
additional proxies for the spy, that is, if they aren't actually CIA agents
anyway.

Naqvi's novel takes this idea of interchangeability another step: not only is
the sovereign's role interchangeable, but so too is the role of *homo sacer*.
Agamben argues that the "sovereign subject" or the rights-bearing citizen
exists as a "two faced being, the bearer both of subjection to sovereign power
and of individual liberties" (Agamben 1995: 124–25). The three friends' differing citizenship status illustrates this two-facedness. Chuck's "got no fucking

rights," according to Grizzly, because he's a Pakistani national. Yet, although bereft of the rights supposedly accorded to an American citizen, Chuck remains vulnerable to American law. He's abandoned by the law and yet subject to it. Jimbo, the sole "bonafide American" (Naqvi 2009: 3), does get a phone call, which he uses to contact his girlfriend, an Upper East Side sort with connections to the governor's office (209). Thus, Jimbo's relation to the law remains subject to the sovereign's decision in the sense that the governor ultimately springs him, not due process. Of the three, AC occupies the most liminal position in that he's an immigrant seeking American citizenship. As the novel presents his circumstances, AC remains in a curious position to any sort of national identity, hence his vulnerability to the state's whims which manifest themselves as drug charges. Although there's no doubt that AC did indeed have the cocaine on him when he was arrested, the novel suggests that the drug charge provides a convenient out for the authorities who roundly misunderstood the three friends' activities in Connecticut. Further, Chuck remains convinced that his two friends suffered the same indignities and humiliations while incarcerated that he did, making the resolutions of Jimbo's and AC's individual experiences somewhat beside the point: they are, like Chuck, *homo sacer*, howsoever temporarily. Though Jimbo emerges from the experience the most "normal," as he intends to marry the girlfriend who proved so helpful in securing his release, none of the friends are indeed all that "secure." Their experiences as Pakistanis in pre- and post-9/11 America illustrate how discourses of national security, such as "If You See Something, Say Something™," initiate Manos's (2004: 140, emphasis added) point, also cited above, about "the *production* of bodies that are removed from the juridical order." Just as Ahmed's notion of the circulation of affect contests the essentialism "Culture Talk" ascribes to the Other, so too does Manos's argument about the production of *homo sacer*: the alleged terrorist's body appears fearsome because of how it's read, and its legible inscriptions result from "the sovereign decision and the subsequent abandonment of the juridical" (Manos 2004: 139). The three friends, who have different relations to the state and, thus, to the law, emerge from their experience with the security state in different ways, forwarding an ambiguity, an uncertainty over who indeed does benefit from the sovereign decision and who suffers from it. Manos recognizes this uncertainty, contending that "the national body is also marked by an *indeterminacy* because it is both intimately coded by the juridical, and yet always maintains its status as potentially the subject of the sovereign decision, always potentially *homo sacer*" (139). Further, given the false circumstances under which Chuck, AC, and Jimbo are incarcerated, *Home Boy* also calls into question the ability to know based on sight, a calling into question that necessarily qualifies the accuracy of any explanation for how the security state "knows" the alleged "terrorist."[3]

Hamid's *The Reluctant Fundamentalist* also focuses on the positions of the sovereign and *homo sacer*. However, rather than tracing lateral interchangeability between those protected and abandoned by the law, as Naqvi's novel does, Hamid's novel marks the symmetry of the sovereign's and the banned person's positions. Agamben argues that:

> the sovereign and *homo sacer* present two symmetrical figures that have the same structure and are correlative: the sovereign is the one with respect to whom all men are potentially *homines sacri*, and *homo sacer* is the one with respect to whom all men act as sovereign.
>
> (Agamben 1995: 84)

Both figures exist inside and outside the law; the difference in their positions lies in the fact that the sovereign exercises power over others, while *homo sacer* is vulnerable to all exertions of power. In labeling these two figures "correlative," Agamben also emphasizes their interdependence, stressing how the order the sovereign maintains by suspending the law only has coherence due to *homo sacer*. Thus, the state of exception, which results from the sovereign decision, produces not just the body of *homo sacer* but also the bodies of the sovereign and the citizens, as well—a point, I argue, that Chuck and his friends illustrate. Going a step further, acknowledging the sovereign and *homo sacer*'s symmetry matters, then, because it emphasizes an ambiguity that stretches vertically along the hierarchy that posits the sovereign at the top, the citizen just below, and *homo sacer* at the very bottom. Hamid's novel seizes on this verticality and inverts it in order to contest the legitimacy and inviolability of the sovereign decision.[4] At the same time, this challenge to the legitimacy of the sovereign decision also impacts subjects' relation to the law and their occupation of space, since to challenge the sovereign's power is to challenge how the state of exception operates. That is, in Ahmed's terms, a change in one's relation to the law or how one occupies the state of exception also alters the "politics of mobility, whereby mobility of some bodies involves or even requires the restriction of the mobility of others" (Ahmed 2004b: 70). In contrast to the spatial constraints under which Chuck labors in *Home Boy*, Changez, Hamid's protagonist, reclaims an expansive mobility post-9/11. To be clear, *The Reluctant Fundamentalist* does not offer, in my estimation, a new political vision or a new relation to the law, which is the potentiality Agamben (1995: 187) identifies at the end of *Homo Sacer* as a site of agency; rather, Hamid's novel switches up who occupies what role and, in Harleen Singh's (2012: 32) terms, "repudiates the subduing of the Other"—moves that force the sovereign and the citizen to "see" the world through the eyes of the banned figure.[5]

Hamid's Changez and Naqvi's Chuck have a lot in common: both serve as character and narrator in their respective fictions; both travel to the US to attend university and, after graduating, attempt to find employment there; both experience pre- and post-9/11 New York as Pakistani Muslim males; and both ultimately return to Pakistan. Further, like Chuck, Changez engages in narratorial play that destabilizes the certainty the visual purportedly affords, which, again, addresses an illiteracy that results in a misreading. As I suggest above, the difference between the two novels is the consequences of the ambiguity they forward. In *Home Boy*, the ambiguity that results from the friends' differing outcomes highlights a pervasive vulnerability to the sovereign's decision. Ambiguity in *The Reluctant Fundamentalist* refuses this vulnerability and, instead, re-directs it toward the sovereign himself.[6] This redirection matters, because it functions as a form of resistance to the discursive and material violence inflicted upon the post-9/11 *homo sacer* through "Culture Talk," sanctioned detentions, and drone attacks, for instance.

Several instances of Changez's narratorial play rely on the visual. Through the use of a second-person address, Changez as narrator controls what readers learn about his life in the US and Pakistan, about the present circumstances that bring him into contact with an unnamed American interlocutor, and about his own motives, even as he pulls the reader—who occupies the same position as the unnamed American—into the story. Readers see what Changez sees. This style of narrative address thus plays with both the identificatory and revelatory processes so common to conventional espionage fictions. Readers cannot help but respond to Changez's direct address and be strung along by his narratorial pacing. Moreover, Changez hints rather persuasively from the start that his American interlocutor is likely either a spy, a contractor, or a Special Forces Operator. Changez notices his interlocutor's physical appearance, for instance: he has "short-cropped" hair and an "expansive chest—the chest I would say, of a man who bench-presses regularly, and maxes out well above two-twenty-five" (Hamid 2007: 2). In addition, Changez draws attention to the man's *"bearing"* (2, emphasis in original). Changez's interest in the man's bearing signals to the reader that the stranger has a commanding presence, that he occupies space in a confident way, which says a lot given that the two meet in Anarkali, a thriving Lahori bazaar. Other hints appear throughout: the man may have a gun holstered under his jacket (139); the American has indeed seen combat (129); and he definitely relies upon a satellite phone, which suggests that his need to stay in contact with whomever far outstrips any regular cell phone's capacity (115). The revelation of these little details, many of which call attention to what Changez observes, enhances the reversal of conventional expectation, as readers never peer inside the American's perspective, as they would were the novel a straightforward example of spy fiction. This denial of perspectival glimpse posits Changez in the protagonist's role, positioning him as the novel's affective center.

Similarly, Changez reveals a heightened self-awareness of his role as narrator that plays with the visual. He proclaims to the American that, in contrast to life in America, being in Pakistan requires "a different way of *observing*" (Hamid 2007: 124, emphasis in original). In effect, Changez introduces a different visual economy through this comment and his overall narratorial perspective. Several metafictional insertions expand the metaphorical import of this economy. In response to what appears to be a direct question from the American about the specifics of one of the stories Changez shares, the latter comments, "I cannot now recall the man's particulars [...]; to be honest, I cannot now recall many of the details of the events I have been relating to you. But surely it is the *gist* that matters" (118, emphasis in original). By italicizing *"gist,"* Changez as narrator draws attention to how the word appears, a clever way of re-investing appearances with significance determined in alternative or Other ways. That is, Changez is asking the American and the novel's readers to accept appearances, but he's asking that these appearances be accepted on his terms. Such a request implicitly acknowledges that appearances can signify in multiple ways, while it also implies Changez's dis-satisfaction with how appearances have been construed prior to his own telling of these stories. Changez works this very insight about the significance of seeing—literally and metaphorically—into his own biography. He labels his desire to succeed in the US as "blinders" (93); their removal results in "the sudden broadening of my arc of vision" (145). All of these narratorial and biographical revelations seek to unstick the associations that link "Pakistan," say, with "terrorist" by insisting upon another way of seeing.[7]

Changez's position as the novel's affective center, as well as his advocacy of an alternative visual economy, contribute to the novel's inversion of the state of exception. How bodies appear and take up space matter a great deal in this inversion. The novel's third sentence announces Changez's physical appearance. As he approaches the American in Anarkali, Changez says, "Excuse me, sir, but may I be of assistance? Ah, I see I have alarmed you. Do not be frightened by my beard: I am a lover of America" (Hamid 2007: 1). Instantly, the novel invokes what Ahmed would call the cultural politics of fear by foregrounding the visual: "see" ties to "alarmed"; Changez's beard implicitly signifies threat, otherwise his declaration of love for America would make no sense. With these associations—and Changez's interest in inverting them—established at the very start at the novel's most contemporary temporary plane, i.e. post-9/11, the novel makes Changez's beard a broader trope that signifies a refusal of the sovereign's decision, a resistance to the "bare life" of the *homo sacer*. Prior to this scene, however, are several occasions when Changez desires to be swathed in Americanness, something he thinks possible due to his educational pedigree and his prestigious job. Upon landing his job, for instance, Changez relays, "I did not think of myself as a Pakistani, but as an Underwood Samson trainee, and my firm's impressive offices made me *proud*" (34, emphasis in original). Later, while on assignment in Manila just before 9/11, Changez speculates that his "Pakistaniness was invisible, cloaked by my suit, by my expense account, and—most of all—by my companions" (71). His speculations and imaginings meet an abrupt end after 9/11. At the Manila airport, Changez is "escorted by armed guards into a room where I was made to strip down to my boxer shorts." This experience leaves him "uncomfortable in my own face; I was aware of being under suspicion [...]" (74). Notably, at this time, Chan-gez is clean shaven and looking every bit the young professional, save for his brown skin. His admission of discomfort *in his own face* signals one of the narrative's breaking points in that this moment (along with a few others, including his role playing with his unrequited love, Erica) could well have resulted in Changez internalizing the status of *homo sacer*, as Chuck did.

Instead, Changez wrests control over what his appearance signifies away from "armed guards" and the plane's other passengers who have "looks of concern" on their faces (Hamid 2007: 74). This control manifests itself in Changez's beard. Grown during a visit to Pakistan, Changez's beard functions, by his own admission, "perhaps, [as] a form of protest on my part, a symbol of my identity; or perhaps I sought to remind myself of the reality I had just left behind [in Pakistan]" (130). The beard becomes a declaration of self-determination, of living by other rules. Whereas Changez previously desired his Pakistaniness to be invisible, now, bearded, he confesses that he "did not wish to blend in with the army of clean-shaven youngsters who were my coworkers" (130). By distinguishing himself from his coworkers via his physical appearance, Changez understands that he's provoking a response:

> More than once, traveling on the subway—where I had always had the feeling of seamlessly blending in—I was subjected to verbal abuse by complete strangers, and at Underwood Samson I seemed to become overnight a subject of whispers and stares.
>
> (Hamid 2007: 130)

Willfully, Changez makes himself vulnerable to this abuse and ignominy not because he feels deserving of this degradation but precisely because he refuses to see his beard as deserving of this debasement. His comments to the American underscore this point: "It is remarkable, given its physical insignificance—it is only a hairstyle, after all—the impact a beard worn by a man of my complexion has on your fellow countrymen" (Hamid 2007: 130). Changez deliberately torques the cultural politics of fear to assert his own identity and to refuse his relegation to "bare life."

The agency Changez exercises by maintaining his beard not only amounts to a refusal of "bare life" but also opens the possibility of a broader reversal of roles. Visual cues remain crucial to this possibility. Throughout his interactions with the American, for instance, Changez calls attention to the man's demeanor. After being alarmed by Changez's beard from the very start, the American "seem[s] worried" about the waiter who serves them at a café in Anarkali, an unease that persists throughout their meal (Hamid 2007: 5, 108). The arrival of tea makes the American "suspicious," perhaps because he fears an upset stomach, which Changez graciously suggests, or perhaps because "it has been *poisoned*" (11, emphasis in original). As Changez escorts the American back to the Pearl Continental near the close of the novel, the former exhorts the latter that he "would do well to relax," even though "those men," including the waiter, "are now rather close, and yes, the expression on the face of that one [...] is rather grim" (183). All mentions of the American's comportment contribute to a sense that he is not in control of his surroundings— an unusual occurrence, it would seem, given how Changez remarks upon his commanding *"bearing"* at their initial acquaintance. In effect, over the course of the conversation, the American appears to have slipped from the sovereign's role—if the reader thinks it possible that the American is CIA or a contractor or Special Ops meaning to do Changez harm—to that of *homo sacer*. He now inhabits the state of exception as one who's been abandoned by the law, one over whom others, including Changez and the group of men who have followed them to the Pearl, act as sovereign.

The novel develops this possibility of role reversal through an extended prey/predator metaphor, too, which also hinges upon the idea of being seen or evading being seen. Early in the novel, Changez uses this metaphor as a way to remark upon the American's discomfort:

> I hope you do not mind my saying so, but the frequency and purposefulness with which you glance about [...] brings to mind the behavior of an animal that has ventured too far from its lair and is now, in unfamiliar surroundings, uncertain whether it is predator or prey!
>
> (Hamid 2007: 31)

By calling attention to the American's "unfamiliar surroundings," Changez begins to lay the groundwork for his argument that in Pakistan one needs to observe differently, which is the novel's way of insisting upon appearance's alternative set of significations. Other occurrences of the prey/predator metaphor leave unresolved which role the American occupies. In one instance, he's clearly prey: load-shedding causes the lights in Anarkali to go out momentarily, an event that makes the American "jump as though you were a mouse suddenly under the shadow of a hawk!" (Hamid 2007: 60–61). At another point, Changez affiliates himself with the American, claiming that both are "swift enough to escape detection and canny enough to hunt among a crowd" (63). Elsewhere, the American, likened by Changez to a fox, appears the predator (77). As this metaphor floats through Changez's narration, it highlights both characters' vulnerability to the sovereign decision, to be sure, and it resonates with the extension of the sovereign's power via predator drones. At the same time, however, it also mounts a resistance to the order that would posit the American as the inviolable sovereign. Changez works within the same structure but opens the possibility of his acting as sovereign.

This act of resistance found in Hamid's *The Reluctant Fundamentalist* begins to address what several critics have identified as a shortcoming in Agamben's theorizing of the state of exception. As I note above, Agamben closes *Homo Sacer* with a critique of Foucault's *History of Sexuality*, which posits, in Agamben's view, "'a different economy of bodies and pleasures' as a possible horizon for a different politics" (Agamben 1995: 187). Less sanguine, Agamben councils caution with respect to the formulation of "a different politics," because the "'body' is always already a biopolitical body and bare life, and nothing in it or the economy of its pleasures seems to allow us to find solid ground on which to oppose the demands of sovereign power" (187).[8]

Ewa Ziarek (2008: 89), among others, offers a corrective to Agamben's insufficient attention to questions of resistance. Drawing on early twentieth-century hunger strikes by British suffragists, Ziarek identifies in that form of protest a "collapse of the distinctions between sovereignty and bare life, will and passivity, potentiality and actuality, the struggle for freedom and the risk of self-annihilation" (100). Most significant for Ziarek is the fact that these historical hunger strikes are "generated from below, rather than imposed by a sovereign decision" (102). Changez's actions as narrator and character do not fully replicate the collapse Ziarek sees occurring in her own extra-fictional example. However, Changez does refuse passivity, effectively reworking the structure from the ground up; the novel's ambiguous conclusion, approached in part via the prey/predator metaphor, does "collapse the distinction between sovereignty and bare life," even if it doesn't offer an entirely different political model. These reversals of the state of exception's verticality, coupled with the lateral interchangeability made evident in *Home Boy*, belie efforts to impose the sovereign's power without challenge and, thus, correct a metaphorical illiteracy that would otherwise naturalize the sovereign order, i.e. present it as inviolate and ineluctable.

The introduction of ambiguity, contingency, reversals, and resistance into this contrapuntal reading of post-9/11 Pakistani and American espionage fictions also contests, through the play with the representation of the alleged "terrorist," the power to know or conquer the Other. By messing with the "see something" of the "If You See Something, Say Something™" campaign, the Pakistani fictions re-frame the "say something" that is occurring in the American texts. *Home Boy* and *The Reluctant Fundamentalist* unmoor certainty by asking readers to "see" something else when they "look" at Chuck and Changez. In doing so, they also contest the relegation of these characters to "bare life." Carrying that impulse over to the reading of the post-9/11 American spy fictions entails an inquiry into the power of explanation these novels claim as they represent the "terrorist" in fixed terms. Thus, where the Pakistani fictions unsettle, the American ones nail down, insisting upon the legitimacy and necessity of labeling the alleged "terrorist" *homo sacer*. Clymer argues that, as a genre, espionage fiction "transforms an incomprehensible political situation [...] into [...] ethical categories," wherein the "political aspects of these books [may] simply [be] fillers for the more significant ethical opposition" (Clymer 2003: 14). As an acts of transformation, these explanations claim to know— or in some instances, to be completely befuddled over—why the "terrorist" does what he does. However, as Clymer suggests by his identification of "ethical categories" as the end goal of these transformations, the power to explain relies upon pre-existing extra-fictional paradigms that help the novel and, thus, the reader organize the Other and the threat he embodies with little need to understand the political and historical forces informing international and global relations. These paradigms frequently involve "Culture Talk" and the positing of an unbridgeable divide separating "us" from "them," two moves that contain and conquer the Other.

As a result, explanations of the "terrorist" connect to but don't entirely replicate the revelatory process that is so central to establishing both the spy and his proxy as a conventional spy novel's affective center. In relation to the spy, the revelatory process illustrates his authority. The explanations that accompany the "say" aspect of Homeland Security's campaign illustrate the interpretive paradigms that bolster this authority, paradigms that explain "difference" rather than encourage a more complex understanding of difference, to hearken back to the distinction made in the Introduction. The emphasis on marked bodies or the visual in Naqvi's and Hamid's novels exemplifies this point: these characters' bodies are "read" as dangerous, because the collective fear and suspicion stoked by "If You See Something, Say Something™," for instance, invoke a way of interpreting these bodies. Manos (2004: 136) contends that security discourses "creat[e] a field of knowledge about the identity and behavior of the dangerous body"—a field, I would add, constructed via the interpretive paradigms featured in these post-9/11 American spy fictions. The Pakistani texts disrupt this field, insisting that there are other ways to read.

These alternative reading practices bear implications for the production of identity. According to Clymer (2003: 19), terrorist violence "becomes a powerful cultural site from which individuals draw meanings, social narratives, and political connections that simultaneously cement ties to some people while drawing lines of alienation and discontinuity from other groups." Less a matter of knowing with certainty anything about the Other and more about consolidating in-group identities, the dynamic Clymer describes also suggests that any understanding of "terrorists" and their acts undergoes filtering processes that may or may not be attentive to the specifics of situations and histories. That "alienation and discontinuity from other groups," which often appears as a "clash of civilizations," thus results from the interpretations of events rather than from inherent incompatibilities. Significantly, both the reading approaches that depend on explanation's paradigms and those that the Pakistani texts begin to sketch focus on the body, on what's right there, but the former moves toward closure, while the latter suggests the possibility of multiple meanings. Whether via "Culture Talk" or an emphasis on vast divides, the power of explanation following from the "say" of Homeland Security's campaign functions as an interpretive paradigm, a way to provide "security" in the sense of a solid epistemological and even ontological base. The impulse operating here runs counter to the reversals and inversions, the lateral moves and re-hierarchizations, occurring in the Pakistani texts. In other words, these efforts to provide "security" manifest an illiteracy, a necessary failure to read or a misreading of the Other.

"Say" explanations premised upon a notion of a vast division between the West and the Muslim world feature prominently in the post-9/11 American spy fictions, and all of them manifest some degree of "Culture Talk." Indeed, the power of the revelatory process I discuss in Chapter 2, as well as the spy's and proxy's relation to place and its inhabitants, which I discuss in Chapter 3, lay the foundation for the post-9/11 US novels' representation of the "terrorist."

The thread of "Culture Talk" runs through all three of these discussions. In Chapter 2, "Culture Talk" manifests in Pashtunwali, for instance, the cultural code of conduct many of these novels deploy to account for why the Pashtun characters do what they do. That is, Pashtunwali determines their actions, illustrating Mamdani's (2004: 18) point that "Culture Talk" insists upon Muslim conformity. "Culture Talk" emerges again in Chapter 3's discussion of the spy's and proxy's tendency to essentialize people and place, which in the representations of Pakistanis, involves endlessly framing them as liars and seeps outward from an "understanding" of people to a knowing of place. With respect to how these post-9/11 US spy fictions represent the "terrorist," each type of "say" explanation I discuss relies in some measure on a dynamic of "Culture Talk." Most prominent among them is the tendency within "Culture Talk" to divide Muslims into "good" and "bad" categories, a move that, at times, reduces complexity to perpetuate fear and, at others, (inadvertently) introduces an ambivalence that confuses more than clarifies.

One of the most reductive examples of such "say" explanations can be found in Coes's *Coup d'État* (2011). For instance, Aswan Fortuna, the Lebanese "terrorist" who finances the elections of the Iranian and Pakistani leaders and seeks vengeance on Dewey Andreas, Special Forces Operator and the novel's hero, proclaims definitively, "'If there's one lesson from the past two decades, it's that Islam is borne on a river of jihad. Violence is a necessary means to the end'" (Coes 2011: 17). That end includes the destruction of Hindu India, Jewish Israel, and all-around-baddie America. Nearly comically two-dimensional, Fortuna, as Dewey's nemesis, embodies the worst excesses associated with the figure of the militant Islamist terrorist. Moreover, the novel does nothing to balance this portrayal of Islam as a violent religion. Indeed, the Pakistani President repeats this characterization, proving great minds think alike. Framed as physically hideous and morally evil, Omar El-Khayab, radical cleric and democratically elected President of Pakistan, insists, like his benefactor Fortuna:

> "The hardest lesson I had to teach my students at the madrasa was about the need for violent jihad [...] That the violence was somehow necessary in order to create a world *without* violence. That Islam, that most beautiful and peaceful of religions, demanded that the blood of the infidel be spilled across the earth in order to wash away the filth of the past."
>
> (Coes 2011: 62–63)

As El-Khayab continues, he makes clear that the difficulty of this lesson lay in the fact that he was merely a teacher stuck behind the walls of the madrasa, not a warrior who would know the glory of jihad (Coes 2011: 63). These "say" explanations that posit Islam as inherently violent stitch together several tropes. First, they frame Islam-as-violence as an offensive move, as if those carrying out this violence are engaged in imperialist expansion. Further, these "say" explanations gloss over cultural, political, and historical identities, preferring to connect this violence almost exclusively with the religious. El-Khayab's memories of the madrasa emblematize this connection. Also, by having two different characters espouse such similar worldviews, the novel suggests that thoroughly "bad" Muslims exist. Such Muslims are beyond reason and deserve the (defensive) violence the US visits upon them. The interpretive paradigm that results entertains no nuance or suggestion that violence may erupt for any number of other reasons or that the ascription of evil or "badness" to Muslims may serve other ideological and political purposes. In many ways, such clear-cut distinctions set the tone for many of the other "say"-oriented explanatory types found in the post-9/11 US espionage novels.

"Why do they hate us?" serves as another particularly common variation of "say" explanations. Like the "Islam is violent" explanation, "why do they hate us?" requires a clear and irreconcilable difference between "us" and "them." Moreover, deployments of this explanation function in several seemingly contradictory ways, introducing victim's discourse, opacity, arrogance, and transparency. Yet, no matter the route, the invocations of this "say" explanation lead to an interpretive paradigm that starts with the assumption of hierarchical relations much like those that exist between the sovereign and *homo sacer*. In Ignatius's *Blood Money* (2011), for example, Ted Yazdi, the fictional White House Chief of Staff, can't quite crack the "why do they hate us?" riddle. Frustrated and confused, Yazdi complains to the head of a new-fangled CIA operation, "'These crazy fuckers still want to kill us, don't they? These Pakistanis and Waziris and whatever the hell else. Why do they hate us so much? [...] We're trying to make them happy'" (Ignatius 2011: 59). The use of pronouns here creates distance while also inviting readers to identify with the "us." Notably, Yazdi's comments go even further in their characterization of the "they": he uses "whatever" instead of "whoever" in his list of national and ethnic group names. Yazdi's pronoun choice dehumanizes the "Pakistanis and Waziris," as well as any other group that may "want to kill us." Such dehumanization clearly inserts a distance between "us," who are human, and "these crazy fuckers," who are closer to things. Notably, Yazdi's professed inability to understand why "these crazy fuckers" hate us inserts an opacity into the power of this "say" explanation. Such an inability to know only serves to reinscribe the great divide separating the "us" and the "them." Though not an example of the "why do they hate us?" explanation, Colin MacKinnon's *Morning Spy, Evening Spy* also features another "say" explanation that relies on opacity. In reference to Pakistanis of all stripes—alleged "terrorists," drug lords, Inter-Services Intelligence, and the average person—Carl Lindquist, MacKinnon's fictional Chief of Station in pre-9/11 Islamabad, proclaims, "The Paks are just being Paks—who knows why they do anything?" (MacKinnon 2006: 117). MacKinnon's novel, published in 2006, ends on the morning of 11 September 2001, just before the first plane hits the North Tower of the World Trade Center. This chronology allows *Morning Spy, Evening Spy* to critique the intelligence failures the novel suggests led to the events of that day. Thus, in one respect, the novel argues for change. Yet, by having Lindquist diagnose Pakistani opacity *before* 11 September 2001, *Morning Spy, Evening Spy* also suggests a troubling continuity: namely, the ongoing opacity of Pakistanis. Just as *Blood Money* does, MacKinnon's novel contributes to an interpretive paradigm that sets up a divide and adds to it the idea that this divide exists regardless of time or circumstance.

Other examples of the "why do they hate us?" explanation reinforce and develop many of these same ideas. In Ignatius's *Body of Lies* (2007), the third-person narrator reveals the interior thoughts of the novel's spy hero, Roger Ferris, who accepts that "they hate us," even if he doesn't explain why. He understands from the time of the 1991 attack on the World Trade Center that "[t]hese people hate us. They don't want to negotiate anything. They want to kill us" (Ignatius 2007: 61). These three sentences convey Ferris's convictions in stark terms. Further, with their simple grammatical structures, they stand out from the rest of the paragraph, which is comprised of compound and complex sentences. Just as in *Blood Money*, the use of the pronouns "they" and "us" also emphasizes the divide between the groups, pulling readers squarely into the "us" camp in the process. By connecting form and content, Ferris, via the narrator, presents radical Muslim hatred and desire to kill Americans as an indisputable fact, plain and simple. Ferris draws this conclusion from "reading Arabic newspapers and visiting mosques" (Ignatius 2007: 61), activities which the novel presents as sufficient to arrive at authoritative declarations such as "they hate us." The narrator presents Ferris's thoughts about the 1991 attack as a memory Ferris indulges in his post-9/11 present. Thus, much like how *Morning Spy, Evening Spy* implies that Pakistanis exist in an ongoing state of sameness across time, *Body of Lies* implies that Ferris's understanding about 1991 carries over without change or reconsideration to his present-day explanation for why 9/11 happened, which is, very simply, that they hate us. Later in the same novel, Ed Hoffman, Ferris's boss at the CIA, supplements Ferris's explanation for why they hate us by assuring Ferris that the terrorists in Pakistan will fall for their plan because "[t]hey think we're Superman. That's why they hate us so much" (Ignatius 2007: 261). Such high national self-regard highlights the absence of the specifics and nuances of history and global politics already so evident in Ferris's unreflective assumptions that newspapers and sermons are all the sources he needs to understand the Other across place and time.

As these examples suggest, "why do they hate us?" functions as an explanation unto itself. In instances when the question nearly obviates an answer, such as with Yazdi's comments, one detects a plaintive tone. Yazdi claims to be unable to comprehend why the "Pakistanis and Waziris and whatever the hell else" can't accept the happiness the US is trying to bring them. There's a trace of the righteous victim in this perspective. Hoffman's Superman comment aligns with Yazdi's point about happiness in that both posit that what the US appears to be and has to offer represents the best the world can hope for. Thus, arrogance meets victimization. Ferris's certainty that they do indeed hate us, derived as it is from his forays into Arabic newspapers and Friday sermons, adds an element of transparency to what is surely a complicated series of connecting and conflicting histories, migrations, cultures, and social codes. In other words, Ferris's knowingness simplifies the alleged "terrorist," an epistemological move that contains the Other on the way to conquering him. This simplification, this certainty that "they hate us," when coupled with the strains of arrogance and victimization also found in the "why do they hate us?" explanation, invokes an interpretive paradigm that automatically slots the "us" and the "them" in relationships that can evolve into sovereign/*homo sacer* with relative ease.

Another type of "say" explanation seeks to neutralize the stark oppositions between "us" and "them" by implying that the "terrorists" who hate us suffer under the burden of perceived marginalization. Yet, this explanatory paradigm reinscribes the binary and fails to promote any alternative understanding; through a derivative characterization that divides "good" and "bad" Muslims, this explanation allows the association between "Islam" and "terrorist" to remain intact. Elleke Boehmer's definition of the "terrorist" provides a prime example of this "say" explanation. Boehmer (2009: 148) frames the "terrorist" as bearer of a type of exceptionalism: "a terrorist may be broadly defined as one who believes that their case is exceptional (they have been unconscionably denied), and that the odds stacked against them are so high that desperate action alone will suffice." This definition hinges on the oppositional, a stand-off characterized by a lethal combination: perceived disadvantage and desperation. The exceptionalism on display here bears a closer resemblance to conventional deployments of the term in an American context than to the state of exception I've been discussing in the sense that what these conventional sorts of exceptionalisms share is a conviction that specific groups deserve extra or special consideration. Further, just like the specific trajectory traced from victim's discourse to savior's role that I discuss in relation to the spy, this definition imposes a narrative framework on the "terrorist" that asks to be read in similar terms. In other words, Boehmer's definition familiarizes the Otherness of the "terrorist" by invoking an explanatory framework that keys in on the same terms and tropes found in the US's own preferred self-defining narratives. Literacy here relies upon rendering the Other in the Same's likeness. Or, in reverse, an illiteracy potentially remains if the Other exists in terms outside those this definition allows. Moreover, as definition, Boehmer's assertion makes a knowledge claim, howsoever "broadly," and, in using "desperation," this definition implicitly casts the "terrorist's" emotional state of mind, suggesting in turn a personalized reading of that figure's motives. In Gargi Bhattacharyya's (2008: 56) view, explanations that locate terroristic motivation in the "personal psychological distress of the individual" "represent a particular and highly significant strategy of othering." Once again resembling the die that casts the spy, this explanation for the "terrorist" involves affective appeals—both positive and negative—and resonances, based on "belief," rather than encouraging an examination of historical, political, economic, and cultural conditions that give rise to materially based antagonisms. As a result, the working out of who does and does not subscribe to these beliefs proves more difficult than Boehmer's definition suggests. When does "desperation" go from being an historically and politically produced collective condition to an internalized subjective affliction? Can we distinguish between assessable claims, on the one hand, and affective appeals and resonances, on the other? This type of "say" explanation produces an interpretive paradigm based on ambivalence rather than certainty but doesn't recognize that basis. It confuses analysis, since it requires a stark opposition and its undoing, relegates some to the margin while embracing others of the same type into the fold. Its frequent deployment in post-9/11 US spy fictions thus confuses more than clarifies as it reverts to a binaristic structure it purports to move beyond.

MacKinnon's *Morning Spy, Evening Spy* takes a page from Boehmer's definition, appearing to advocate the idea that desperation born of "feeling that their lives are out of their control," of "poverty and humiliation," motivates young Muslims to become "terrorists" (MacKinnon 2006: 189–90). Amjad Afridi, the character expounding this explanation, is himself a Pakistani Muslim, a fact that, the novel suggests, grants his assessment extra authenticity. These comments appear in a section of the novel in which Afridi educates Paul Patterson, the spy-protagonist; Afridi is the native informant. Labeling "Muslim countries" "beggars among nations," Afridi further holds that "all these places are so poor, so weak, so ignorant" (189). Backwards, outside, or left behind by time, "Muslim countries" have no agency. Afridi's account holds out no possibility that these countries could be something else, something other. By no means uncommon in both fictional and extra-fictional accounts of what motivates "terrorists," Afridi's rendition holds particular power, because it appears to come from an insider, one capable of translating this foreign culture so that it is legible for the likes of Paul Patterson, the spy trying to protect his country. Yet, Afridi's middle position, his role as translator, reinforces rather than breaks down the divide between "Muslims" and the rest of the world.

Alex Berenson's *The Faithful Spy* (2006) similarly wants to have both the "desperate" and the acceptable, the "bad" and the "good" Muslim. The novel's protagonist, John Wells, a CIA agent under deep cover in al-Qaeda even before 11 September 2001, represents the possibility of an acceptable Islam. In part an element of his job and later a profound aspect of his character, Wells converts to Islam, because the religion "touched him in a way that Christianity never had. [... H]e loved the Koran's exhortation that men should treat one another as brothers and give all they could to charity" (Berenson 2006: 26). This portrayal of Islam as a principled and generous religion aligns with much "war on terror" discourse that frames the US's interests in Muslim cultures as efforts to extend human rights, gender equality, etc., thereby suggesting that Muslims would be amenable to the "good" the US represents. Further, Wells's religious belief domesticates Islam in the sense that it makes the religion appealing and accessible to someone raised in a Judeo-Christian tradition. Yet, alongside this declaration of religious devotion, Wells, via the third-person narrator, also admits that he thinks:

> Islam's biggest strength was its greatest weakness [...] The religion's flexibility had made it a cloak for the anger of men [... who] wanted to take the religion back to the seventh-century desert. They couldn't compete in the modern world, so they would pretend it didn't exist. Or destroy it.
>
> (Berenson 2006: 27)

A clear line of demarcation, Wells's assessment of Islam's strengths and weaknesses lays the groundwork for the assigning of Muslims to "good" or "bad" categories. Even more, Wells accounts for why "bad" Muslims are "bad": they can't "compete in the modern world." Wells's relegation of these "bad" Muslims to pre-modern times, as well as his disclosure of what draws him to Islam to begin with, confirm Mamdani's (2004: 18) claim that "Culture Talk," in part, frames Islam as "premodern," which actually means "antimodern." Moreover, representations of "antimodern" Muslims "are productive of fear and preemptive police or military action" (18). The line from "antimodern" and "bad" Muslim to *homo sacer* is a short one. Noting that this "antimodern" strain of "Culture Talk" is "deeply reminiscent of tracts from the history of modern colonization," Mamdani goes on to argue that this discourse also can't read the agency these "bad" Muslims may be exercising. That is, "[t]his history stigmatizes those shut out of modernity as antimodern [and they are so] because they resist being shut out" (19). The suggestion here is that "history" can't imagine any group not wanting to be "modern" in whatever prescribed fashion that would involve. Thus, the "antimodern" exists as diametrically opposed to the "modern," fixed against "us," illustrating how the "good"/"bad" distinction upholds implacable divides.

Berenson's novel represents Wells's nemesis, the al-Qaeda operative Omar Khadri, as the "bad" Muslim, and, as it develops how the novel frames the "bad" Muslim, this characterization highlights the ambivalence underlying Boehmer's explanation. Partially responsible for 9/11 and now, in the novel's present, actively plotting attacks across the US, Khadri:

> fully expected that one day the world would know his name, his real name. Biographers and historians would examine his life. But if they were looking for a traumatic event, something they could "blame" for clues to his "crimes," they would be disappointed, he thought.
>
> (Berenson 2006: 79)

Ostensibly deflecting and deflating psychological and individualized explanations for his behavior by denying the existence of a "traumatic event" that catalyzes his terrorist activities, Khadri, the narrator reveals, nonetheless needs to "prove his strength to the world, and his father," a Pakistani immigrant who settled in Birmingham, UK (Berenson 2006: 79). Indeed, Khadri's father exerted more influence on him than he cares to admit, as "the lash of his father's belt" taught the young Khadri "not to disagree" (79). Such an authoritarian environment, the novel suggests, spurred Khadri's interest in learning "how strong men forced their will on the weak" (79), and militant Islam provides Khadri with the proper outlet for the disgust he feels over "the moral corruption around him [in the UK], drug taking and homosexuality and pleasure seeking at all costs" (80). Vehemently not a fanatic, Khadri understands that "rational men like him were needed to win this war [against the US]" (80). In the few paragraphs the novel devotes to sketching Khadri's childhood, his adherence to Islam, and his political discipline, it implies causal links between Khadri's lack of paternal love and his need to exert his own power as a Muslim over non-believers. Not only do these links belie Khadri's own insistence that "biographers and historians" would find no "traumatic event" to "blame" for his actions, but they confuse motivations, allowing "desperation" to be at once both a product of familial dysfunction and perceived cultural injustice. Although Wells later suffers a crisis of faith, which leaves him rather agnostic in his religious convictions, the novel's early depiction of the sincerity of his faith, especially with its emphasis on what aspects of Islam Wells finds most appealing, enforces the notion that certain Muslims can integrate, can be like "us." At the same time, Wells's diagnosis of Islam's "greatest weakness" also posits the view that Islam may well be commandeered by the "bad" type of Muslim, the Khadris of the novel (and the world), which leaves both these "bad" Muslims and Islam itself as stuck in the "them" side of the "us"/"them" binary.

Ignatius's *Body of Lies* takes up the "good" Muslim aspects of this "say" explanation, and, just as Berenson's novel does, shows how it confuses rather than clarifies, reinforces divides rather than bridges them. Sami Azhar, a CIA agent who's assisting in Ferris's continent-spanning operation, "'used to be a quant on Wall Street. He was born in Egypt, but he came to America to go to graduate school [...] He got very rich working for a hedge fund. So rich that he decided to give something back to his adopted country'" (Ignatius 2007: 140). As the embodiment of the traditional immigrant success story, Sami acquires education and wealth in the US and is then duly grateful. His demonstrated reciprocity suggests that Sami transfers his loyalty, along with his skills, to a country that accepts him fully without prejudice or obstacle. Sami's post-9/11 attitudes reinforce this notion that he has joined the American fold, as his boss at the CIA explains:

> "Sami used to do some fancy freelance work for the agency and the NSA [National Security Agency] in the nineties, helping us understand the crazies who were trying to kidnap his religion. But after 9/11 he realized that the world had gone off its rocker and that only a complete idiot would keep working for a hedge fund. As a Muslim, he felt a special responsibility to help stop the loonies."

> (Ignatius 2007: 140)

By emphasizing that Sami worked for the covert services before 11 September 2001, this depiction of Sami's patriotism suggests that US post-9/11 foreign policy has not been a "war on Islam." Such a suggestion is common in 9/11 discourses of fear, or so says Sara Ahmed (2004a: 132), in that it appears to decouple the association of "Islam" or "Muslim" with "terrorist." Yet, the proximity "Muslim" with "loonies" in this passage, for instance, implicitly re-"sticks" the association. As Ahmed explains, "The slide of metonymy can function as an implicit argument about the causal relations between terms (such as *Islam* and *terrorism*) within the making of truths and worlds, but in such a way that it does not require an explicit statement" (Ahmed 2004a: 131–32). Indeed, what's really at stake in this characterization of Sami Azhar is the exemplification of the "good" Muslim in contrast to the "desperate" sorts who turn into "terrorists."

Despite Sami's patriotism, however, the segregation of Muslims into "good" and "bad" categories confuses as much as it explains. The distinction appears to bear explanatory power, as I've been arguing, because it helps enforce/reinforce the idea that only "desperate" Muslims become "terrorists." As Mamdani (2004: 15) contends, such a distinction "would allow for the embrace of the ['good'] and the casting off of the ['bad']." One consequence of this division, then, is that it justifies relegating the "bad" to the status of *homo sacer*. Yet, as Mamdani also points out, the division "masks a refusal to address our own failure to make a political analysis of our times" (16). Here's where the confusion comes in. By deeming some Muslims "good," hence acceptable, and others "bad," thus threatening, this distinction contributes to an interpretive paradigm that muddies political, cultural, and religious identities. Of course, identities are complex, and they encompass all these vectors and more at once. Yet, in a post-9/11 context, there's an impulse to read political identities as religious ones, otherwise we would have no need to declare that Islam is or isn't a violent religion. Mamdani expands on this point: in a post-9/11 context, "unless proved to be 'good,' every Muslim was presumed to be 'bad.' All Muslims were now under obligation to prove their credentials by joining in a way against 'bad Muslims'" (Mamdani 2004: 15). By recognizing that the "good"/"bad" distinction imposes evidentiary requirements on all Muslims, Mamdani highlights the narrowness of understanding or the illiteracy operating when such a distinction holds sway. That is, rather than analyzing the impulse behind creating the distinction or the complexities attendant to any articulation of individual and collective identity, the need or demand that "good" Muslims prove themselves to be so reads these individuals' religious identifications as the most or only salient aspect of their subjectivities, as if being "Muslim" means adherence to "Islam" solely. In many ways, Malini Johar Schueller's point regarding Giorgio Agamben's treatment of the Muselmann in Primo Levi's holocaust writings is germane here, too.[9] Schueller (2009: 244) takes issue with Agamben's failure to interrogate how the figure of the Muselmann "appears in the language of the [concentration] camp." Far from neutral, Schueller claims, the use of the term "Muselmann" to signify, in Agamben's words, "a being from whom humiliation, horror, and fear had so taken away all consciousness and all personality as to make him absolutely apathetic" (Agamben 1995: 185), calls forth orientalist tropes the recognition of which by Agamben and others would alter the terms of the former's insights and enhance our abilities to analyze the state of exception (Schueller 2009: 244). Similarly, the call for "good" Muslims to declare their loyalty to "our" side flattens the contexts that produce the "good"/"bad" designations to the extent that Muslims can only be read as dangerous or mollified figures.

This array of "say" explanations, the range of which covers "why do they hate us?" to an impulse to separate "good" from "bad" Muslims, invokes interpretive paradigms which, in a sense, precede any fictional representation of the "terrorist." That is, these explanations connect to broader trends in representation that exist outside any individual work of fiction. In effect, these "say" explanations gain momentum from how we're taught to "see." The Department of Homeland Security's "If You See Something, Say Something™" campaign crystallizes these links between the seen and the said, a chain of interpretive practices that I've argued Naqvi's and Hamid's novels attempt to break. Both of these Pakistani fictions take up the figure of the "terrorist" in decidedly visual terms in an attempt to refuse the categorizations and invert the power relations so crucial to the putative inviolability of the sovereign's ban. With this emphasis on the seen, these Pakistani novels' representation of the "terrorist" amounts to the most explicit instance of my metaphorization of "propaganda by deed" in the sense that they amplify the spectacle to introduce an alternative visual economy. Throughout the preceding chapters, I've read shallowly and contrapuntally, juxtaposing post-9/11 Pakistani and American texts, to trace how the former identify the illiteracies readily apparent in the latter. In doing so, I've demonstrated how all these post-9/11 fictions influence new developments in the espionage genre and highlighted through my readings of the Pakistani texts how the popular deployment by the American texts of the genre's stock conventions makes acceptable the logic that renders the place of the Other into a state of exception and relegates the Other to "bare life." By way of a conclusion, in the final section I use the insights gained through these shallow readings to identify the illiteracies operating in media and US government representations of the extra-fictional drone program.

Notes

1 Elleke Boehmer (2009: 145), among others, makes the point that in seeking to protect the "homeland" through these localizing measures, the US "implies that terror is everywhere, and hence it must constitute the primary mode of sovereignty of the counter-terroristic state itself."

2 See also Heidemann's (2012: 292–93) reading of this scene, which focuses on the three friends' efforts to de-center the two brawlers' presumed superiority.

3 Bidhan Chandra Roy (2011: para. 20) argues, in contrast, that Naqvi's portrayal of Chuck encourages American audiences to embrace Chuck's secularity and other "like" features and, thus, fails to "broach [any] meaningful political and cultural differences between the US and many Muslims in the world."

4 Leerom Medovoi (2011: 646) implicitly acknowledges this inversion when he argues that Hamid's novel "personif[ies] an America confronted with an opportunity to grasp for the first time the actual nature of its relationship to Pakistan."

5 Roy (2011: para. 22) notes Changez's interest in the visual, too though not to the extent I do. He also argues that Changez's actions are reactionary, prompted only by the US's rejection of him.

6 In chapter 7 of *Contemporary Pakistani Fiction in English: Idea, Nation, State*, I argue that *The Reluctant Fundamentalist*, as well as several other post-9/11 Pakistani fictions, reverse the migrancy trope common to postcolonial studies. One of the hallmarks of this reversal, I contend, is these fictions' emphasis on the potential brutality of the migrant experience. That argument complements the points I make here regarding how Hamid's novel upends the sovereign's hierarchy.

7 Peter Morey argues that Changez delivers these revelations in a "hoax confessional" style that parodies the rigid categorization that accompanied American post-9/11 binaristic thinking (Morey 2011: 136). For Morey, this parody leads to a disorienting "deterritorialization" for the reader, a point consistent, I think, with my own interest in how Agamben's notion of "dislocating localizations" demonstrates the provisional security enjoyed by those who benefit from the sovereign's power (Morey 2011: 136).

8 See de la Durantaye's *Giorgio Agamben: A Critical Introduction* (2009), especially pages 234–38, for a survey of critiques of Agamben's cautiousness.

9 Schueller (2009) cites both Agamben's *Homo Sacer* and *Remnants of Auschwitz* in her critique. See pages 184–85 in Agamben's (1995) *Homo Sacer* for his initial discussion of the figure of Levi's Muselmann.

Conclusion
Drones

In January 2011, Raymond Davis, a CIA contractor who once worked for Blackwater, a private military company, allegedly killed two Pakistani men in a crowded Lahore intersection in broad daylight. Immediately after the incident, the US government identified Davis as a "diplomat" rather than as connected to the CIA. Weeks later, though, the Barack Obama Administration owned up, a move that, according to Mark Mazzetti, "shed an unflattering light on a post-Sept. 11 reality: that the C.I.A. had farmed out some of its most sensitive jobs to outside contractors—many of them with neither the experience nor the temperament to work in the war zones of the Islamic world" (Mazzetti 2013b). With that confession made, Leon Panetta, the CIA Director at the time, called upon then Pakistani Ambassador to the US Husain Haqqani to ask for help in getting Davis out of the Lahore prison in which he'd been held since the incident (Mazzetti 2013b). Mazzetti's source for a report of this meeting claims that Ambassador Haqqani replied, "'If you're going to send a Jason Bourne character to Pakistan, he should have the skills of a Jason Bourne to get away'" (Mazzetti 2013b). The Americans did eventually broker a deal with the Pakistanis, and Davis returned to the US. Mazzetti's recounting of these protracted events surrounding Davis's presence in Pakistan troubles the CIA's license to kill by illustrating an extreme case, suggesting that not only does a civilian contractor have no business performing some of the agency's "most sensitive jobs," but neither does the agency itself. Indeed, the reinstatement of the agency's ability to use lethal force—and to extend this ability to its contractors—following President Gerald Ford's 1976 ban on CIA assassinations marks the "war on terror" as a significant turning point in how the US wages war and in the CIA's role in such conflicts. As Scott Shane remarks in a *New York Times* article on drone usage, "Only in the drone era has killing terrorism suspects become routine" (Shane 2013b). Apparently carrying on with that routine, a day after Davis's departure, the CIA launched a drone attack on a meeting of suspected militants in the Federally Administered Tribal Areas (FATA) of Pakistan. This attack gave rise to strenuous disagreements between the Pakistanis and Americans, as well as between different groups within the US government; the "militancy" of the dozens of men killed in the attack was at issue (Mazzetti 2013b).

The timing of the Davis episode, which unfolded in the early months of 2011, coincided roughly with the Navy SEALs raid on Osama bin Laden's Abbottabad compound in May 2011, as well as with a NATO airstrike in November of that year that killed twenty-four Pakistani soldiers (Living Under Drones 2012: 15). Effectively, this string of events sensitized relations between the US and Pakistan to an unprecedented degree, and the uptick in drone usage—one *New York Times* article reports that there was a "sharp rise" in drone strikes in the first two years of President Obama's first administration, with 117 drone strikes in 2010 being the current high-water mark (Shane 2013b)—lit a match in this tinderbox. Thus, this Raymond Davis episode constellates several dynamics I have been discussing throughout the preceding chapters: the expansion of sovereignty to encompass the spy's proxies and the state of exception that results. Pointedly, given Haqqani's comment, fiction plays a role in drawing our attention to these events that occur right before our eyes, thanks to the immediacy of media coverage.

Phrased in the terms I have been using throughout these discussions, Davis stands in for the latest end point of sovereign power. Further, the CIA's drone attack, following so close on the heels of the resolution of the Davis affair, nearly begs to be read as a vehement reassertion of sovereign power. "Reading" the situation matters in another way, as well, given Ambassador Haqqani's reference to Robert Ludlum's fictional spy, Jason Bourne, embodied on the Cineplex screen three times over by American actor Matt Damon. Haqqani's recourse to fiction—or, really, just the possibility opened up by Mazzetti's reporting that Haqqani mentioned Jason Bourne—highlights the central purpose of this concluding chapter: namely, to identify the "illiteracies" on the surface of non-fictional representations of US–Pakistani relations, especially when they involve spies and "terrorists." In effect, my aim is to explore what is gained when shallow reading as an interpretive approach—honed throughout the preceding chapters via the metaphorization of the Pakistani novels as instances of "propaganda by deed"—takes as its object not only genre fiction but also newspaper and magazine articles, and even government reports, on the US government's ongoing drone program. This conclusion, then, addresses the last of the interconnected issues I outlined in the Introduction: to assess how analyses of literary narratives concerned with espionage and terrorism can reshape our approach to non-fictive representations of the same concerns. I take my lead from Melani McAlister, whose groundbreaking study, *Epic Encounters*, shows that:

> cultural productions help make meanings by their historical association with other types of meaning-making activities, [including] the actions of state policymakers [...] This suggests that we might ask less about "what texts mean"—with the implication that there is a hidden or allegorical code to their secret meaning—and more about how the texts participate in a field, and then in a set of fields, and thus in a social and political world.
>
> (McAlister 2005: 8)[1]

The texts I examine below, thus, enter into the discursive field already populated by the post-9/11 Pakistani and US espionage novels that make up the bulk of this study. Rather than privilege the non-fictive texts as more "real" than the fictive ones, my point is to identify where phenomena such as affective appeals, "Culture Talk," the sovereign ban, and *homo sacer* jump genre. The coincidence of these phenomena's appearance, then, within both fictive and non-fictive representations, made visible precisely through the contrapuntal reading of the Pakistani novels' appropriations of espionage conventions, promotes a more "literate"—but, perhaps, no less contentious—understanding of the Other.

Relatedly, this turn to non-fictive texts brings my analyses into conversation with similar investigations in the fields of "critical criminology" (Iadicola 2009–10: 110) and International Relations (IR). Scholars working on the "war on terror" in these two social science disciplines similarly invoke Agamben, for instance, as they concern themselves with questions of sovereignty. By considering the sovereign ban as constitutive of belonging, as securing benefits to those not banned, Claudia Aradau and Rens van Munster seek to alter the common criminological view that "exceptional politics *overwrites* the law" to a recognition of how this very politics actually "*underwrites* the law" (Aradau and van Munster 2009: 688–89). Further, like Sunaina Maira (2009: 632–33) and Halit Mustafa Tagma (2009: 410) from their own disciplinary perspectives, Aradau and van Munster (2009: 693–94) identify how the state of exception "relegate[s] the [Other] to the category of cultural and even racial infrahumanity." Aradau and van Munster's neologism "infrahumanity" focuses on the moral values assigned or denied to those under or benefitting from the sovereign's ban. IR scholars key into this unequal valuation to contest paradigms in their field that do not recognize, for instance, that "presumptions [...] about what it means to be human, to be rational and desiring, are historically and culturally produced, and are thus 'particular' rather than universal" (Seth 2013b: 23). An acknowledgment of this particularity matters for several reasons, including that it challenges any impulse to lock Others into history's "waiting room" (Seth 2013a: 9) and emphasizes how the legitimacy of nations and peoples "is the product and effect of centuries of interaction of the West with its others" (Tagma 2009: 427). Together, these reasons justify Christine Helliwell and Barry Hindess's appropriation of anthropologist Johannes Fabian's concept of the "denial of coevalness" for IR theory. In anthropology, this denial refuses to see "those being studied [as] exist[ing] in the same time period as the anthropologist. Instead, the contemporary Other is transmuted into our past/primitive ancestor" (Helliwell and Hindess 2013: 71). Helliwell and Hindess's interest in Fabian's concept resonates with Mahmood Mamdani's notion of "Culture Talk," which similarly functions to lock Muslims into an Islamic past, creating the perception that Muslims are "petrified" in a foundational revelatory moment several centuries past (Mamdani 2004: 18). No good comes from this denial, as Helliwell and Hindess (2013: 79) further argue: "we should expect perceived temporal backwardness to be associated with a perceived lack of real individuality and thus to be accorded a lower value." In essence, the analyses I have conducted throughout this study enact these insights shared by criminologists and IR scholars, illustrating how reading novels by the Other in direct relation to those by authors presenting familiar worldviews can crystallize "real world" dynamics and make visible their unjust and material consequences.

The "sort of" covert US drone program, playing out in the skies above Pakistan and other locations, represents perhaps the most (in)visible "real world" example of the issues I've been discussing throughout the preceding chapters. My use of the qualifier "sort of" before "covert" is a deliberate oxymoron, for covert operations require complete invisibility in order to be entirely secret. Yet, as Pakistanis have known for well over a decade and as Americans can't help but be aware since roughly 2009, the CIA's (and the US Armed Forces') use of weaponized drones in Pakistan, a geographic location outside the theater of active hostilities, has been an ever-present facet of everyday life for people living in Pakistan's FATA, a region adjacent to Pakistan's Northwest Frontier Province and situated along the Durand line, that porous border with Afghanistan. As Matt Delmont (2013: 157) argues, given the escalating use of drones in Pakistan, "the war [on terror] is both omnipresent and routinely hidden from view." In effect, then, the CIA's drone program encapsulates a paradoxical (in)visibility: the US government acknowledges the program—a new development—but says little about it, while those affected by drone strikes, as well as several human rights and media organizations, offer concrete "proof" of the strikes' human costs. As Declan Walsh (2013), another *New York Times* journalist, reports, the US State Department can neither confirm nor deny these costs, especially in terms of civilian casualties, because such information is classified. In a perverse twist of the Department of Homeland Security's "If You See Something, Say Something™" campaign, with respect to the CIA's drone program, the US government would rather nothing all that penetrating were said, no matter how much people have seen. Another way of formulating this point is to observe that only some people's testimony or witnessing matters, and, given the major critical points I've explored here, including the sovereign ban, the state of exception, and *homo sacer*, this possibility may not be too far off the mark. Such discursive constraints necessitate an examination of what non-fictional sources do say about the drone program. Scrutinizing these "says" brings into focus the attitudes shaping representations of the program, its "value" and its costs, and identifies the illiteracies operating in this discursive field.

In this chapter, I extend the critical impulse issued by my analyses of the post-9/11 Pakistani fictions featured throughout this study to examine a number of non-fictional sources, such as articles from *The New York Times* and various other periodicals, as well as US government documents, including a speech by John Brennan when he was President Obama's Chief Counterterrorism Advisor, a letter to Senator Patrick Leahy written by Attorney

General Eric Holder, and a leaked US Department of Justice White Paper on the use of drones to kill US citizens abroad. My aim is to demonstrate the pertinence of the key concepts I've drawn upon in previous chapters to the analysis of these non-fictional representations of US–Pakistan relations to see whether and how these concepts manifest in the justifications for and objections to drone usage. In line with what I've been suggesting thus far, the trope of (in)visibility figures prominently in these representations, and I refine this trope further to highlight how these various publications cast (in)visibility as transparency; as both ordinariness and affective identification; and as a type of knowledge claim through deployments of "Culture Talk." Set forth by these subtopics, the trope of (in)visibility familiarizes drone usage for an American audience, though this familiarity differs both in kind and degree from how those populations targeted by drone surveillance and violence in Pakistan and elsewhere experience this expansion of US sovereignty. This familiarizing process matters, because it normalizes the expansion of sovereignty drones represent, as well as the related consequences, such as rendering places into states of exception and reducing those places' inhabitants into beings protected by no laws, but subject, nonetheless, to the sovereign's power.

These non-fictional sources employ transparency as a metaphor for understanding the drone program, in part acknowledging the obvious point that the US is using these unmanned aerial vehicles for surveillance and military purposes. In a 30 April 2012 speech published on the Council of Foreign Affairs website, John O. Brennan, who was serving as the Assistant to the President for Homeland Security and Counterterrorism at the time, asserted that "transparency" about the US's counterterrorism efforts, including the use of drones, aligned with the nation's "values" "upon which our democracy depends." Similarly, in a 22 May 2013 letter, Attorney General Eric Holder insists that the Obama Administration promotes "an unprecedented level of transparency into how sensitive counterterrorism operations are conducted." Like Brennan, Holder sees these efforts to be more open as "consistent with our laws and values." This recognition of the obvious extends even to Pakistani discussions of US drone activity. In April 2013, for instance, former Pakistani President Pervez Musharraf admitted to CNN that his government gave its consent to US drone strikes, though he qualified the number to "two or three times only" (*Tribune* 2013). Such an open admission, howsoever blunted, confirms the suspicions Mirza Shahzad Akbar raises in his *New York Times* op-ed, where he states that in Pakistan, people "widely believ[e]" that their government offers "tacit consent" and perhaps even on-the-ground intelligence to aid the CIA in their strikes (Akbar 2013). These representations of government officials owning up to the use of drones appear to be taking responsibility for the program and to be encouraging the public to trust that drone usage occurs within a legal and ethical framework that reinforces American democracy. In effect, these representations ask audiences to engage in a sort of shallow reading, to understand the entire drone program based upon what they see or what they "see" through reports of drone strikes. Visibility thus becomes a sanctioned full knowing.

However, this full knowing is, in fact, an illusion and this type of shallow reading is inadequate largely due to government efforts to render invisible additional evidence that remains stubbornly detectable. Musharraf's hedge of "two or three times only" requires a credulous audience to be believed given, as Nic Robertson and Greg Botelho report, the Pakistani government's "repeated denunciations of a program they long claimed the United States was operating without their approval" (Robertson and Botelho 2013). Further, in the US government's official statements, assurances of "transparency" fudge any secure sense of what the American public and the broader global audience can know about the CIA's use of weaponized drones. For example, despite his claim to "reject the notion that any discussion of [drone use] is to step onto a slippery slope that inevitably endangers our national security," Brennan also insists that the administration needs to strike a "delicate balance between secrecy and transparency" (Brennan 2012). Such a both/and rhetorical move inadvertently justifies media portrayals that cast the drone program as there and not there, so to speak. Declan Walsh, for instance, frames drone use as veiled by a "curtain of secrecy" and as "largely shielded from public oversight and outside scrutiny" (Walsh 2013). Further, Walsh characterizes the back-and-forth between the US and Pakistan over which nation is responsible for any particular drone strike as mired in "murkiness." A 2012 report entitled "Living Under Drones," co-authored by Stanford's International Human Rights and Conflict Resolution Clinic, and NYU's Global Justice Clinic, states plainly that the US government's efforts to inform the public about the drone program have failed "to ensure basic transparency" (Living Under Drones 2012: vii). These we said/they said proclamations create a tense discursive field wherein every surface ends up being multivalent, as the drone strikes and the conditions of their possibility bear cultural, political, military, technological, and economic dimensions.[2] Audiences know they "see," but, with drones, what they're "seeing" is explicitly partial. What results, in other words, are competing "scopic regimes," a phrase Derek Gregory (2011: 190) uses to refer to "a mode of visual apprehension that is culturally constructed and prescriptive, socially structured and shared." Thus, what appears as a complete knowing from one perspective may end up looking like an "illiterate" representation when analyzed alongside additional perspectives or, as I have attempted to do throughout this book, when analyzed in light of what the post-9/11 Pakistani fictive appropriation of shared tropes and themes emphasizes. Efforts to understand, then, must account for what comes into view from a variety of shifting locations. These efforts comprise the sort of shallow reading I've been advocating.

Thus, I want to situate this chapter's analyses within such a context of illiteracy in order to highlight how these non-fictional representations of drone usage familiarize audiences with this program—a move that, I contend, makes the use of weaponized unmanned aerial vehicles acceptable to segments of the population who are not "living under drones," to borrow the title from the Stanford-NYU joint publication. Stunning mundaneness (given the subject matter) stands in as one of the primary features of the familiarizing process as it emerges from the non-fictional sources I examine. Writing as recently as March 2013, Declan Walsh of *The New York Times* seems to parody representations of drone attacks in Pakistan. Walsh shares, for instance, that media reports of recent "run of the mill" attacks "carried typical" and "common-sounding details" (Walsh 2013). Of course, parody has no place in a straightforward journalistic piece, leading to the conclusion that accounts of drone attacks have themselves become a genre. Once conventionalized in the ways Walsh appears to be suggesting, reports of drone attacks follow a script and frame material reality in ways that align with the audience's pre-set expectations. As in all forms of representations, that is, conventions make possible certain ways of understanding while also forestalling others. Beyond implying that the representations of drone attacks follow a format, Walsh's specific characterizations also indicate a certain ordinariness, as if the events themselves—to say nothing of the conditions that make the drone attacks as events possible—are so unexceptional that they don't warrant specification.

A similar sense of ordinariness operates in Anna Mulrine's (2008) article entitled "Warheads on Foreheads," which appeared in *Air Force Magazine*. The title's pithiness presumably speaks to the desirability of drone usage. Just the possibility that a US-based publication would employ such aphorisms already suggests a level of acceptability. Several colorful and action-oriented photographs accompany the article and set off in a curious fashion the author's framing of the physical location from which drone pilots operate. These pilots work "in a nondescript dun-colored building squirreled away in a remote base in a Midwest state that does not wish to be identified" (Mulrine 2008: 44). While, on the one hand, the article's accompanying visuals play up the spectacular nature of combat and the effects the drone's weapons have, the article's text downplays what can be seen, on the other. The actual building where the pilots launch their strikes is nothing special; indeed, authorities "squirrel" it away, out of sight, so that nobody notices it. Yet, this penchant for secrecy lies strangely next to the building's "nondescript" appearance. In this vision, the most unremarkable sights ostensibly downplay their own remarkableness. The building's very ordinariness suggests that it doesn't disrupt the proximate populations, much like, through their familiarity derived from repetition, conventionalized representations don't disrupt an audience's expectations.

Other representations couple this mundaneness with affective appeals, adding an identificatory aspect to the familiarizing process and mirroring this impulse to identification I've argued occurs in the literary representations of spies. In an article entitled "Robots at War: The New Battlefield," published in 2009 in *The Wilson Quarterly*, Peter Warren Singer attempts to humanize the use of robots, including drones, in armed conflicts, and these efforts result in representations that create a visual of a certain kind of "average" American life. Mirroring my own interest in iRobots with which I opened this book, Singer, too, starts his article with reference to this Boston-based company, noting that it is situated in a "drab office park," "across from a Macaroni Grill restaurant and a Men's Wearhouse clothing store" (Singer 2009: 31). In the midst of this most banal vision of American suburbia, Singer holds, "the future of war is being written" (31). Much like the "dun-colored building" from which drone pilots launch their strikes, iRobot's headquarters could be conducting their lethal business anywhere in the US, but, by highlighting how the company sits in a "drab office park" not far from chain restaurants and shops, Singer's representation quells the threat this company's business poses to its proximate populations. Indeed, Singer points out that military personnel refer "affectionately" to some of the smaller robots as R2-D2, the anthropomorphized droid from George Lucas's *Star Wars* movies.[3] This article takes another step toward affective identification by presenting the drone pilots as regular *parents* doing their day's work—that is, if their lives are standard issue middle to upper-middle class. According to Singer, Americans now live in a time "when a pilot could 'go to war' by commuting to work each morning in his Toyota to a cubicle where he could shoot missiles at an enemy thousands of miles away and then make it home in time for his kid's soccer practice" (Singer 2009: 32). The article concedes that these adjustments are psychologically jarring, because they blur the line between combat mode and the domestic life that is supposedly outside the realm of militarized violence, a point that resonates with the fictional blurring of lines between the clandestine and citizens' realms. Further, Singer goes on to worry about the public's detachment from warfare should it become roboticized to an even greater extent (45–48). This worry focuses on the possibility that the American public may be more willing to wage war because doing so involves so little human risk (48). What this point misses, however, is that right now drone usage entails significant human risk for those "living under drones." Yet, insofar as Singer's representation of drone pilots renders them into a cookie cutout version of American life—a life in which one drives a Toyota and works, Dilbert-style, in a cubicle and punches the clock in time to get to one's child's soccer practice—it also invites a generalized identification through which readers can see some (idealized?) version of themselves or their neighbors. This ordinariness, complemented by the settings both Singer and Mulrine invoke, neutralizes the issues involved in drone usage, lessening the stakes and increasing its acceptability.

Familiarization through framing drone usage as mundane and as the day job of someone "just like me" encourages a certain understanding of what the program is about. The mundaneness of the technology—or the centers at which the technology is deployed—seems to suggest that little harm comes of drone strikes (beyond the intended damage, that is).[4] The invitation to identify with the drone pilots renders the program acceptable, because we're reluctant to judge anyone who is like "us" as acting immorally. Further, as the representation of the spy makes clear, we tend to view domestic lives as outside of history and politics. This tendency toward the separation of spheres operates explicitly in Singer's (2009: 34) assessment that drone pilots have to contend with the "psychological disconnect of being 'at war' while still dealing with the pressures of home." In the scenario Singer sketches, the cognitive dissonance arises because the two spheres shouldn't and don't ordinarily come into contact. The familiarity born of identifying with the bourgeois lifestyles of these drone pilots—at least as they're represented—helps the broader public navigate such disconnections and, potentially, share in the under-standing of how difficult it is to juggle the "work/life balance," all the while failing to recognize the inter-relation of the two spheres or, in other terms, how those enjoying this bourgeois lifestyle are benefiting from—and not abandoned by—the sovereign's rule.

"Culture Talk" complements these aspects of the familiarizing process. With its essentializing tendencies, "Culture Talk" helps develop a sense of knowing the Other. The "Living Under Drones" report identifies Pashtun-wali, "an ethical code and 'system of customary legal norms'" (Living Under Drones 2012: 22), as one reason that the people inhabiting the FATA may be extending hospitality to insurgents and terrorists:

> This duty to provide hospitality to all may create complications where it leads civilians to provide shelter to armed non-state actors, not out of support for their cause, but to fulfill a fundamental duty.
>
> (Living Under Drones 2012: 23)

Mark Mazzetti's (2013a) reference to Pashtunwali invokes a similar framework, as he concludes that "treachery" may result should "Waziri tribesman [...] hand over the foreign fighters" to Pakistani or American spies. Even though these two sources actively call into question the US's drone program, they nonetheless draw upon the same revelatory process evident in the post-9/11 US espionage fictions to account for, to know, to predict how FATA's inha-bitants have acted or will act. That is, by relegating these people's actions to a strict adherence to custom or tradition, both the "Living Under Drones" report and Mazzetti's article lock these people into a determinism dictated by a past that seems to an American audience to be out of joint. In these repre-sentations, the inhabitants of FATA have little agency, much less political convictions of their own. Their culture explains everything. That even sources critical of the US's drone program employ "Culture Talk" shows how domi-nant this type of discourse is. Moreover, this recourse to "Culture Talk" facilitates a sense of full knowing, (inadvertently) reinforcing the "scopic regime" constructed by the transparency tropes appearing throughout these non-fictive representations of the US's drone program.

Many of the points I have brought up thus far resonate with the analyses I have derived from reading the Pakistani novels' appropriation of elements central to the post-9/11 US spy fictions. The (in)visibility tropes and the impulse toward familiarization, for instance, mirror the identificatory and revelatory processes that endow the figure of the fictive spy with both credibility and authority. As I've argued, the spy needs to possess these characteristics so that his attitudes toward the Other and the places the Other occupies—be those places an entire nation or just the portable "space" that surrounds the Other's body—become acceptable, unassailable even. The nonfictive sources I have been discussing similarly bank upon the familiarization process to shore up the legitimacy of US sovereignty over Other bodies and places. Just as the fictional spy's affective appeal helps readers accept his attitudes, thereby implicating those same readers in the fiction's implicit worldview that separates the domestic and romantic, for instance, from the political and historical, these non-fictional sources expand the sphere of sovereignty to include and implicate *certain* ordinary citizens. The expansion of sovereignty also involves legitimizing the location of the state of exception, as well as the identification of those peoples vulnerable to the sovereign's ban. In this vein, sovereignty first expands to include Americans. Brennan (2012) claims that US citizens "are sovereign," because the nation is a democracy. Moreover, Brennan speculates: "I think the American people expect us to use advanced technologies [...]" Speculation and expectation serve as the bulwarks of action, in Brennan's public formulation, a coupling that situates American citizens—but not *all* American citizens—as both enforcers and benefactors of the sovereign's law. Similarly, Mirza Shahzad Akbar (2013) calls upon the "Pakistani government [to] exercise its duty to protect the lives of its citizens" from US drone attacks. Just as the "Living Under Drones" report and Mazzetti's investigative journalism draw upon "Culture Talk" in the same ways that the US spy fictions do, here Akbar's argument relies upon the discourses of citizenship and rights to act as an intervention into drone usage. Both examples expand the sovereign's power even beyond what the US spy fictions do, so that it now also encompasses—and not just benefits—ordinary citizens, both Pakistani and American, too. Put another way, both examples must use the framework premised upon the deployment of the sovereign ban.

If anything, these non-fictive sources clearly display the structures and strictures of this framework. Brennan (2012) states plainly that the government's "counterterrorism efforts are rooted in, and strengthened by, adherence to the law, including the legal authorities that allow us to pursue members of al-Qa'ida—including U.S. citizens—and to do so using 'technologically advanced weapons'." While not an act of Congress, the George W. Bush Administration's restoration of the CIA's ability to use lethal force functions as a sovereign decision in the sense Agamben outlines. Indeed, both through executive mandates and legal means, such as Attorney General Eric Holder's careful tracing of case law to support his arguments for the legality of the US using drones to kill US citizens, the US's actions to legitimize the drone program and other strategies in the "war on terror" make visible exactly what Agamben seeks in *Homo Sacer*: namely, the "hidden point of intersection between the juridico-institutional and the biopolitical models of power"

(Agamben 1995: 6). In other words, Agamben asks us to identify how laws themselves, of which the sovereign ban is both a part and beyond, facilitate the creation of states of exception and the relegation of some living beings to the bare life of *homo sacer* and the protection of other living beings who enjoy the benefits of the sovereign's law. The Department of Justice White Paper, obtained in February 2013 by NBC News, illustrates just this intersection of models of power. The White Paper claims that:

> a lethal operation in a foreign nation [outside an active battlefield] would be consistent with international legal principles of sovereignty and neutrality if it were conducted, for example, with the consent of the host nation's government or after a determination that the host nation is unable or unwilling to suppress the threat posed by the individual targeted.
>
> (NBC News 2013: 2)[5]

The mandates of legal discourse aside, this statement basically allows for any incursion into a "foreign nation," regardless of its government's or its people's involvement in "active" hostilities. What bolsters this go anywhere, do anything attitude, according to the White Paper, is Bush's 14 September 2001 Authorization for Use of Military Force (AUMF), which "does not set forth an express geographic limitation on the use of force it authorizes" (NBC News 2013: 3). This AUMF effectively renders *all* geographic regions as subject to the sovereign's law and, thus, the sovereign's ban. Anywhere could become a state of exception and anyone *homo sacer*.

The ramifications of these legal maneuvers grow all the more pronounced given the consequences of the US's incursions into territories not part of active war zones and the lives ended or disrupted by these drone strikes. The first of these points—incursions into regions not part of active war zones— illustrates how laws and historical relations create actual states of exception. Significantly, in the Pakistani context, the US concentrates its drone strikes in FATA. Mazzetti's (2013a) identification of this location as the US's "laboratory for the targeted killing operations" is more than just tactical. Rather, history plays a role in FATA's vulnerability. As many journalists and scholars note, FATA is a region outside of Pakistani law where only the Pakistani President is sovereign (Living Under Drones 2012: 23). As Ian Graham and Majed Akhter contend, given the Frontier Crimes Regulations of the British Empire to the present-day constitutional status of FATA, which has simply extended the governing principles operating under the British, the sovereign's word—be he the Empire's "political agent" or the Pakistani President—"is indeed law in tribal areas" (Graham and Akhter 2012: 1498). FATA's unusual legal status within Pakistan, along with the US's argument for its non-geographically bound authorization to use force, show how, in Graham and Akhter's (2012: 1500) view, "drone warfare [becomes] a reality in certain spaces and not others."[6] This region's exceptionalism further bolsters the "value" of drone usage. As the "Warheads on Foreheads" article extols, citing a Colonel in the

US military, drones "provide 'a true asymmetric [weapon] that the enemy cannot detect. There's nothing they can do to defeat the fact that we're watching them 24 hours a day, seven days a week'" (quoted in Mulrine 2008: 37). Such celebratory sentiments illustrate how a region's relegation to the state of exception extends to its people, consigning these inhabitants to the role of *homo sacer*. In this context, the language choices found in the "Living Under Drones" report gain significance. Here, the drones' 24/7 capabilities disintegrate the social fabric: "Drones hover twenty-four hours a day over *communities* in northwest Pakistan, striking *homes*, vehicles, and *public spaces* without warning" (Living Under Drones 2012: vii, emphasis added). Rather than the "enemy," the authors of "Living Under Drones" represent the inhabitants of FATA as "communities" whose domestic and social lives suffer under drones' omnipresence, which stands in metonymically for the sovereign's totalitarian hold. This attempt to highlight the lifeways of the location rather than just the location itself tries to undo the conflation of people to place or to stave off the creep of the state of exception.

The second tangible consequence of the legal maneuverings that justify drone usage involves the lives ended or disrupted by these strikes or, in other words, the production of *homo sacer*. The Obama Administration's use of "signature strikes" helps produce these banned figures. The "Living Under Drones" report explains that "profile" or "signature" strikes are "based on a 'pattern of life' analysis" (Living Under Drones 2012: 12–13). Such analyses focus on "groups of men who bear certain signatures, or defining characteristics associated with terrorist activity, but whose identities are unknown" (quoted in Living Under Drones 2012: 12–13). Stripped of identity and reduced to "defining characteristics," which the report claims "have never been made public" (13), these drone victims manifest what *homo sacer* looks like in the "war on terror" context. According to "Living Under Drones," this profiling logic equates "adult male" with "militant" in the absence of any proof that would challenge this logic. Apparently, teenage boys qualify as adult males in these profiles. As Mark Mazzetti (2013c: 290) reports, "American officials admit it is somewhat difficult to judge a person's age from thousands of feet in the air, and in Pakistan's tribal areas a 'military-aged male' could be as young as fifteen or sixteen." Moreover, by relying upon this logic, the US government, according to Mazzetti, can "claim that the drone strikes in Pakistan have not killed any civilians" (290). Eerily enacting the prejudice and violence fictionalized in the post-9/11 Pakistani novels though with lethal consequence, these "signature strikes" engage both "Culture Talk" and the "scopic regime" I have been discussing. Much like the characters in H.M. Naqvi's *Home Boys* (2009), these "military-aged males" inhabit a portable state of exception in a location that the US and the Pakistani governments already view as exceptional.

These people's vulnerability invites a comparison to other people's security. As I've already noted, some of these non-fictional sources seek to assure audiences of their security through recourse to the notion of the rights-bearing citizen. Brennan's (2012) speech goes so far as to extend sovereignty to such rights-bearing American citizens, at least up to a point. This parceling out of who is secure and who is vulnerable in terms of citizenship has its limits, and Attorney General Eric Holder's letter to Senator Leahy addresses these limits as it outlines when the US government can order a drone strike against a US citizen. According to this letter, the Department of Justice asserts that:

> [b]ased on generations-old legal principles and Supreme Court decisions handed down during World War II, as well as during the current conflict, it is clear and logical that United States citizenship alone does not make such citizens immune from being targeted.
>
> (Holder 2013)

Just as both the US and Pakistani governments rely upon colonial-era Frontier Crimes Regulations to deem FATA exceptional, Holder's letter refers to established practice to justify targeting US citizens. Further, his use of the verb "immune" introduces considerations of what is natural and unnatural.[7] Brennan (2012) uses similar imagery of sick and healthy bodies when he characterizes drones' "surgical precision—the ability, with laser-like focus, to eliminate the cancerous tumor called an al-Qa'ida terrorist while limiting damage to the tissue around it—[as what] makes this counterterrorism tool so essential." Such framings of drones' targets as sick or even "cancerous" excises history and politics, to be sure, and also places value on the "health" of the body that requires this procedure, i.e. the US. The cancer metaphor does even more, by suggesting the unpredictable and uncontrollable ways that cancer can spread and recur. Suddenly, the sovereign's body—and not *homo sacer's*— is the one that is vulnerable, a neat reversal reminiscent of the deployment of victim's discourse in the representation of the spy. The targets may proliferate, as cancer cells do, reinforcing the need for "signature strikes," as well as these more targeted ones, to control the spread of the disease.

The debate over whether the US government can use drones to target US citizens, many have argued, predictably and unfortunately overshadows the bigger point: that there appears to be little concern over the US government targeting Other people. To close the circle I opened in the Introduction, Archbishop Desmond Tutu does raise this objection as he condemns some of the Obama Administration's decisions for how they compromise the nation's "moral standards" and "humanity" (*The New York Times* 2013). From Tutu's perspective, the proposition that only the targeted killings of US citizens merit judicial review sends the message to the rest of the world that "our lives are not of the same value as yours" (*The New York Times* 2013). Tutu's insistence on the humanity of all lives challenges the sovereign's relegation of some people to the state of "bare life" and, thus, to the state of exception. As I noted earlier, however, Agamben seems reticent to embrace any celebratory or liberatory alternative to the sovereign's power, especially any formulation that too quickly embraces the body as the site of subversive potential. Instead,

Agamben (1995: 188) hopes for "the emergence of a field of research beyond the terrain defined by the intersection of politics and philosophy, medico-biological sciences and jurisprudence." I do not intend to claim that any of these critiques of the US drone program constitute this emergence. However, several of these critiques, even when they draw upon the same forms of representation, inadvertently or not, do at least underscore the violence of this intersection. The "Living Under Drones" report, for instance, does reframe drone victims, refusing to succumb to the sovereign ban by insisting upon these people's collective identities as communities even as the report also relies upon "Culture Talk" to explain how and why these people live. Scholars and journalists also expand this effort, pointing out that the CIA's use of lethal force, a capability that exceeds the law, makes of its agents and drone pilots "unlawful combatants" (Solis 2010; Gregory 2011: 190; Feldman 2011: 333). These dissenting voices seek to render the illiterate more literate, to return to the broader impulse that motivates my literary analyses. Insofar as the Pakistani novels I've been discussing take on the figures of the spy, his proxy, and the "terrorist," they also animate, specify, and—importantly—imagine how Agamben's generalized concepts operate in post-9/11 contexts.

Notes

1 Of course, McAlister is interested in US encounters with the Middle East, whereas I will use the impulses forwarded by the Pakistani novels I have been discussing to examine primarily US-based non-fictive representations of Pakistan.

2 The first four dimensions are readily apparent. In addition, as Peter Singer (2009: 36) points out, the sharp increase in drone and robot usage in the "war on terror" has given rise to a "significant military robotics industry," thus illustrating the economic dimension, as well.

3 In fact, Singer (2009) makes literary and pop cultural references throughout his article, inviting readers to understand drone usage through fiction, much like Haqqani's reference to Jason Bourne invites us to think about the Raymond Davis episode through genre fiction.

4 "Laser-like" and "precise" are stock adjectives often found in pro-drone representations. Anna Mulrine (2008: 45) claims that unmanned aerial vehicles provide the US with the capability for "precision attack[s] and intelligence," for instance. Similarly, John Brennan (2012) contends that drone pilots have "laser-like focus."

5 Notably, John Brennan (2012) makes a very similar claim in his speech, delivered months before NBC News released the White Paper, suggesting that the Obama Administration locked down its talking points well before Brennan's nomination for Director of the CIA.

6 Graham and Akhter's (2012) insistence that only "certain spaces and not others" are subject to drone strikes specifies Agamben's ideas about the state of exception in ways that Halit Mustafa Tagma and Malini Johar Schueller would likely endorse.

7 The Department of Justice's White Paper uses almost the exact same language: "[T]he Department does not believe that U.S. citizenship would immunize a senior operational leader of al-Qa'ida or its associated forces from a use of force abroad [...]" (NBC News 2013: 3). Notable here is the Paper's use of the conditional "would," which comes across as less definitive that the version of the statement found in Holder's (2013) letter.

Bibliography

Abu-Lughod, Lila. "Do Muslim Women Really Need Saving? Anthropological Reflections on Cultural Relativism and Its Others." *American Anthropologist* 104(3): 783–90, September 2002.

Adams, Lisa and John Heath. *Why We Read What We Read: A Delightfully Opinionated Journey Through Contemporary Bestsellers.* Naperville, IL: Sourcebooks, 2007.

Agamben, Giorgio. *Homo Sacer: Sovereign Power and Bare Life.* Trans. Daniel Heller-Roazen. Stanford, CA: Stanford University Press, 1995.

——*State of Exception.* Trans. Kevin Attell. Chicago, IL: University of Chicago Press, 2005.

Ahmed, Sara. "Affective Economies." *Social Text* 22(2): 117–39, Summer 2004a.

——*The Cultural Politics of Emotion.* New York: Routledge, 2004b.

——"A Phenomenology of Whiteness." *Feminist Theory* 8(2): 149–68, 2007.

Akbar, Mirza Shahzad. "Obama's Forgotten Victims." *The New York Times*, 22 May 2013. NYTimes.com (accessed 26 September 2013).

Aradau, Claudia and Rens van Munster. "Exceptionalism and the 'War on Terror'." *British Journal of Criminology* 49: 686–701, 2009.

Aslam, Nadeem. *The Wasted Vigil.* Toronto: Doubleday, 2008.

Awan, Muhammad Safeer. "Global Terror and the Rise of Xenophobia/Islamophobia: An Analysis of American Cultural Production since September 11." *Islamic Studies* 49(4): 521–37, 2010.

Bedell, Jeanne F. "A Threatening World: Suspense in Espionage Fiction." *Clues* 13(2): 115–26, Winter 1992.

Bennett, Jane. "Systems of Things: A Response to Graham Harman and Timothy Morton." *New Literary History* 42(2): 225–33, 2012.

Berenson, Alex. *The Faithful Spy.* New York: Random House, 2006.

Berlant, Lauren. "Poor Eliza." *American Literature* 70(3): 635–68, September 1998.

Best, Stephen and Sharon Marcus. "Surface Reading: An Introduction." *Representations* 108(1): 1–21, 2009.

Bhattacharyya, Gargi. *Dangerous Brown Men: Exploiting Sex, Violence and Feminism in the War on Terror.* London: Zed, 2008.

Boehmer, Elleke. "Postcolonial Writing and Terror." Elleke Boehmer and Stephen Morton (eds) *Postcolonial Writing and Terror: A Concise Companion.* Hoboken, NJ: Wiley-Blackwell, 2009, pp. 141–50.

Brennan, John O. "The Ethics and Efficacy of the President's Counterterrorism Strategy." Council on Foreign Relations, 30 April 2012.

Bromley, Roger. "Natural Boundaries: The Social Function of Popular Fiction." *Red Letters* 7: 34–60, 1978.

Butler, Judith. *Precarious Life: The Powers of Mourning and Violence.* London: Verso, 2004.

Cahm, Caroline. *Kropotkin and the Rise of Revolutionary Anarchism 1872–1886.* Cambridge: Cambridge University Press, 1989.

Cawelti, John G. and Bruce A. Rosenberg. *The Spy Story.* Chicago, IL: University of Chicago Press, 1987.

Cilano, Cara N. *Contemporary Pakistani Fiction in English: Idea, Nation, State.* London: Routledge, 2013.

Clymer, Jeffory A. *America's Culture of Terrorism: Violence, Capitalism, and the Written Word.* Chapel Hill, NC: University of North Carolina Press, 2003.

Coes, Ben. *Coup d'État.* New York: St Martin's, 2011.

Cole, Sarah. "Dynamite Violence and Literary Culture." *Modernism/Modernity* 16(2): 301–28, 2009.

Conway, Maura. "Nitro to the Net." *The World Today* 60.8/9 (August–September 2004): 19, 21–22.

cooke, miriam. "Islamic Feminism Before and After September 11th." *Duke Journal of Law and Policy* 9(227): 227–35, 2002.

Crownshaw, Richard. "Deterritorializing the 'Homeland' in American Studies and American Fiction after 9/11." *Journal of American Studies* 45(4): 757–76, 2011.

de la Durantaye, Leland. *Giorgio Agamben: A Critical Introduction.* Stanford, CA: Stanford University Press, 2009.

Delmont, Matt. "Introduction: Visual Culture and the War on Terror." *American Quarterly* 65(1): 157–60, 2013.

Denning, Michael. *Cover Stories: Narrative and Ideology in the British Spy Thriller.* London: Routledge, 1987.

Feldman, Keith P. "Empire's Verticality: The Af/Pak Frontier, Visual Culture, and Racialization from Above." *Comparative American Studies* 9(4): 325–41, 2011.

Fesperman, Dan. *The Warlord's Son.* New York: Vintage Crime, 2004.

Fury, Dalton. *Black Site.* New York: St Martin's, 2012.

Gamal, Ahmed. "Encounters with Strangeness in the Post-9/11 Novel." *Interdisciplinary Literary Studies* 14(1): 95–116, 2012.

Garrison, Arthur H. "Defining Terrorism: Philosophy of the Bomb, Propaganda by Deed and Change through Fear and Violence." *Criminal Justice Studies* 17(3): 259–79, 2004.

Giorgi, Gabriel and Karen Pinkus. "Zones of Exception: Biopolitical Territories in the Neoliberal Era." *diacritics* 36(2): 99–108, Summer 2006.

Graham, Ian and Majed Akhter. "The Unbearable Humanness of Drone Warfare in FATA, Pakistan." *Antipode* 44(4): 1490–509, 2012.

Gray, Richard. *After the Fall: American Literature Since 9/11.* Hoboken, NJ: Wiley-Blackwell, 2011.

Gregory, Derek. "From a View to a Kill: Drones and Late Modern War." *Theory, Culture, and Society* 28(7–8): 188–215, 2011.

Gruber, Michael. *The Good Son.* New York: Henry Holt and Co., 2010.

Hall, Stuart. "Notes on Deconstructing the Popular." Imre Szeman and Timothy Kaposy (eds) *Cultural Theory: An Anthology.* Malden, MA: Wiley, 2010, pp. 72–80.

Hamid, Mohsin. *The Reluctant Fundamentalist*. Toronto: Anchor, 2007.

Harman, Graham. "The Well-Wrought Broken Hammer: Object-Oriented Literary Criticism." *New Literary History* 43(2): 183–203, 2012.

Heidemann, Birte. "'We are the Glue Keeping Civilization Together': Post-Orientalism and Counter-Orientalism in HM Naqvi's *Home Boy*." *Journal of Postcolonial Writing* 8(3): 289–98, July 2012.

Helliwell, Christine and Barry Hindess. "Time and the Others." Sanjay Seth (ed.) *Postcolonial Theory and International Relations: A Critical Introduction*. London: Routledge, 2013, pp. 70–83.

Hemmings, Clare. "Invoking Affect: Cultural Theory and the Ontological Turn." *Cultural Studies* 19(5): 548–67, September 2005.

Hepburn, Allan. *Intrigue: Espionage and Culture*. New Haven, CT: Yale University Press, 2005.

Holder, Eric H., Jr. "Letter to the Honorable Patrick J. Leahy." Office of the Attorney General, 22 May 2013.

Holloway, David. "The War on Terror Espionage Thriller and the Imperialism of Human Rights." *Comparative Literary Studies* 46(1): 20–44, 2009.

Houen, Alex. "*The Secret Agent*: Anarchism and the Thermodynamics of Law." *English Literary History* 65: 995–1016, 1998.

——*Terrorism and Modern Literature: From Joseph Conrad to Ciaran Carson*. Oxford: Oxford University Press, 2002.

——"Novel Spaces and Taking Place(s) in the Wake of September 11." *Studies in the Novel* 36(3): 419–37, Fall 2004.

Iadicola, Peter. "Controlling Crimes of Empire." *Social Justice* 36(3): 98–110, 2009–10.

Ignatius, David. *Body of Lies*. New York: Norton, 2007.

——*Blood Money*. New York: Norton, 2011.

Irom, Bimbisar. "Alterities in a Time of Terror: Notes on the Subgenre of the American 9/11 Novel." *Contemporary Literature* 53(3): 517–47, 2012.

Kaplan, Amy. "Homeland Insecurities: Reflections on Language and Space." *Radical History Review* 85: 82–93, 2003.

Keniston, Ann and Jeanne Follansbee Quinn. "Introduction: Representing 9/11: Literature and Resistance." Ann Keniston and Jeanne Follansbee Quinn (eds) *Literature After 9/11*. New York: Routledge, 2009, pp. 1–15.

Kubiak, Anthony. "Typologies of Terror." *Studies in the Novel* 36(3): 294–301, 2004.

Laqueur, Walter. "The New Face of Terrorism." *The Washington Quarterly* 21(4): 169–78, Autumn 1998.

Latour, Bruno. "Why Has Critique Run Out of Steam? From Matters of Fact to Matters of Concern." *Critical Inquiry* 30(2): 225–48, Winter 2004.

Linse, Ulrich. "'Propaganda by Deed' and 'Direct Action': Two Concepts of Anarchist Violence." Wolfgang J. Mommsen and Gerhard Hirschfeld (eds) *Social Protest, Violence and Terror in Nineteenth- and Twentieth-Century Europe*. New York: St Martin's, 1982, pp. 201–45.

Living Under Drones. "Living Under Drones: Death, Injury, and Trauma to Civilians from US Drone Practices in Pakistan." Living Under Drones, Stanford Law School, 2012.

Love, Heather. "Close but Not Deep: Literary Ethics and the Descriptive Turn." *New Literary History* 41(2): 371–91, Spring 2010.

MacKinnon, Colin. *Morning Spy, Evening Spy*. New York: St Martin's, 2006.

——*The Contractor*. New York: St Martin's, 2009.

Maira, Sunaina. "'Good' and 'Bad' Muslim Citizens: Feminists, Terrorists, and US Orientalisms." *Feminist Studies* 35(3): 631–56, Fall 2009.

Mamdani, Mahmood. *Good Muslim, Bad Muslim: America, the Cold War, and the Roots of Terror*. New York: Pantheon, 2004.

Manos, James Andreas. "Homeland Insecurity and Bodies Born of Crisis." *Radical Philosophy Review* 7(2): 135–48, 2004.

Marr, Timothy. "'Out of the World': Islamic Irruptions in the Literary Americas." *American Literary History* 18(3): 521–49, 2006.

Massumi, Brian. "The Autonomy of Affect." Paul Patton (ed.) *Deleuze: A Critical Reader*. Malden, MA: Wiley-Blackwell, 1996, pp. 217–39.

Mazzetti, Mark. "A Secret Deal on Drones, Sealed in Blood." *The New York Times*, 6 April 2013a. NYTimes.com (accessed 26 September 2013).

——"How a Single Spy Helped Turn Pakistan Against the United States." *The New York Times*, 9 April 2013b. NYTimes.com (accessed 26 September 2013).

——*The Way of the Knife: The CIA, a Secret Army, and a War at the Ends of the Earth*. New York: Penguin, 2013c.

McAlister, Melani. *Epic Encounters: Culture, Media, and US Interests in the Middle East since 1945*. Revised edn. Berkeley: University of California Press, 2005.

Medovoi, Leerom. "'Terminal Crisis?': From the Worlding of American Literature to World-System Literature." *American Literary History* 23(3): 643–59, 2011.

Miller, David. *Anarchism*. London: JM Dent and Sons, 1984.

Morey, Peter. "'The Rules of the Game Have Changed': Mohsin Hamid's *The Reluctant Fundamentalist* and Post-9/11 Fiction." *The Journal of Postcolonial Writing* 47(2): 135–46, 2011.

Morley, Catherine. "'How Do I Write about This?': The Domestic and the Global in the Post-9/11 Novel." *Journal of American Studies* 45(4): 717–31, 2011.

Morrison, Toni. *Playing in the Dark: Whiteness and the Literary Imagination*. New York: Random House, 1992.

Mullen. "iRobot, Do You?" *Mullen.com*, 2011 (accessed 9 February 2013).

——"iRobot SUGV." *Mullen.com*, 2013 (accessed 9 February 2013).

Mulrine, Anna. "Warheads on Foreheads." *Air Force Magazine* 91(10): 44–47, October 2008.

Naqvi, H.M. *Home Boy*. New York: Shaye Areheart Books, 2009.

NBC News. "Department of Justice White Paper," 4 February 2013.

The New York Times. "Drones, Kill Lists and Machiavelli." 12 February 2013. NYTimes.com (accessed 10 September 2013).

Oxford University Press. "appropriate." *Oxford English Dictionary*.

——"Moslem." *Oxford English Dictionary*.

Payne, Kenneth. "Winning the Battle of Ideas: Propaganda, Ideology, and Terror." *Studies in Conflict and Terrorism* 32: 109–28, 2009.

Pease, Donald. "9/11: When Was 'American Studies After the New Americanists?'" *boundary 2* 33(3): 73–101, 2006.

Randall, Martin. *9/11 and the Literature of Terror*. Edinburgh: Edinburgh University Press, 2011.

Ricoeur, Paul. *Freud and Philosophy: An Essay on Interpretation*. New Haven, CT: Yale University Press, 1977.

Robbins, Bruce. "The Worlding of the American Novel." Leonard Cassuto, Clare Virginia Eby and Benjamin Reiss (eds) *The Cambridge History of the American Novel*. Cambridge: Cambridge University Press, 2011, pp. 1096–106.

Robertson, Nic and Greg Botelho. "Ex-Pakistani President Musharraf Admits Secret Deal with US on Drone Strikes." *CNN*, 12 April 2013. CNN.com. (accessed 26 September 2013).

Rothberg, Michael. "A Failure of the Imagination: Diagnosing the Post-9/11 Novel: A Response to Richard Gray." *American Literary History* 21(1): 152–58, 2009.

Roy, Bidhan Chandra. "The Tragic Mulatto Reconfigured: Post 9/11 Pakistani-American Identities in HM Naqvi's *Home Boy* and Mohsin Hamid's The Reluctant Fundamentalist." *Reconstruction* 11(2), 2011.

Said, Edward. *Culture and Imperialism*. New York: Vintage, 1993.

——*The World, the Text, and the Critic*. Cambridge, MA: Harvard University Press, 1983.

Sauerberg, Lars Ole. *Secret Agents in Fiction: Ian Fleming, John le Carré and Len Deighton*. New York: St Martin's, 1984.

Scanlan, Margaret. *Plotting Terror: Novelists and Terrorists in Contemporary Fiction*. Charlottesville, VA: University of Virginia Press, 2001.

Schmid, Alex P. and Janny de Graaf. *Violence as Communication: Immigrant Terrorism and the Western News Media*. London: Sage, 1982.

Schueller, Malini Johar. "Decolonizing Global Theories Today." *Interventions: International Journal of Postcolonial Studies* 11(2): 235–54, 2009.

Sedgwick, Eve Kosofsky. "Paranoid Reading and Reparative Reading, or, You're So Paranoid, You Probably Think this Introduction is About You." *HELDA*. University of Helsinki, 1997.

Sedgwick, Eve Kosofsky and Adam Frank. "Shame and the Cybernetic Fold: Reading Silvan Tomkins." Eve Kosofsky Sedgwick and Adam Frank (eds) *Shame and its Sisters: A Silvan Tomkins Reader*. Durham, NC: Duke University Press, 1995, pp. 1–28.

Sedgwick, Mark. "Al-Qaeda and the Nature of Religious Terrorism." *Terrorism and Political Violence* 16(4): 795–814, 2004.

Seth, Sanjay. "Introduction." Sanjay Seth (ed.) *Postcolonial Theory and International Relations: A Critical Introduction*. London: Routledge, 2013a, pp. 1–12.

——"Postcolonial Theory and the Critique of International Relations." Sanjay Seth (ed.) *Postcolonial Theory and International Relations: A Critical Introduction*. London: Routledge, 2013b, pp. 15–31.

Shamsie, Kamila. *Burnt Shadows*. New York: Picador, 2009.

Shane, Scott. "Debating a Court to Vet Drone Strikes." *The New York Times*, 8 February 2013a. NYTimes.com (accessed 26 September 2013).

——"Targeted Killing Comes to Define War on Terror." *The New York Times*, 7 April 2013b. NYTimes.com (accessed 26 September 2013).

Siddiqi, Yumna. *Anxieties of Empire and the Fiction of Intrigue*. New York: Columbia University Press, 2008.

Singer, Peter Warren. "Robots at War: The New Battlefield." *The Wilson Quarterly* 33(1): 30–48, 2009.

Singh, Harleen. "Insurgent Metaphors: Decentering 9/11 in Mohsin Hamid's The Reluctant Fundamentalist and Kamila Shamsie's Burnt Shadows." *ARIEL: A Review of International English Literature* 43(1): 23–44, 2012.

Solis, Gary. "CIA Drone Attacks Produce America's Own Unlawful Combatants." *The Washington Post*, 12 March 2010. Washingtonpost.com. (accessed 26 September 2013).

Spivak, Gayatri Chakravorty. "Three Women's Texts and a Critique of Imperialism." *Critical Inquiry* 12(1): 243–61, 1985.

Stafford, David. *The Silent Game: The Real World of Imaginary Spies*. Revised edn. Athens: University of Georgia Press, 1991.

Tagma, Halit Mustafa. "*Homo Sacer* vs. Homo Soccer Mom: Reading Agamben and Foucault in the War on Terror." *Alternatives: Global, Local, Political* 34(3): 407–35, 2009.

Takacs, Stacy. *Terrorism TV: Popular Entertainment in Post-9/11 America*. Lawrence, KS: University of Kansas Press, 2012.

Thobani, Sunera. "White Wars: Western Feminism and the 'War on Terror'." *Feminist Theory* 8(2): 169–85, 2007.

Tribune. "'Two or Three Times Only': Musharraf Admits to Allowing Drone Strikes." 12 April 2013. Tribune.com.pk (accessed 26 September 2013).

Tugwell, Maurice. "Terrorism and Propaganda: Problem and Response." *Conflict Quarterly* 6: 5–15, Spring 1986.

US Department of Homeland Security. "If You See Something, Say Something™." Campaign.

Walsh, Declan. "US Disavows 2 Drone Strikes over Pakistan." *The New York Times*, 4 March 2013. NYTimes.com (accessed 26 September 2013).

Westwall, Gary. "One Image Begets Another: A Comparative Analysis of *Flag-Raising on Iwo Jima* and *Ground Zero Spirit*." *Journal of War and Culture Studies* 1(3): 325–40, 2008.

Woods, Brett F. *Neutral Ground: A Political History of Espionage Fiction*. New York: Algora, 2008.

Ziarek, Ewa Płonowska. "Bare Life on Strike: Notes on the Biopolitics of Race and Gender." *South Atlantic Quarterly* 107(1): 89–105, Winter 2008.

Index